LEADERSHIP AND PURPOSE

BY ANDREW M. THOMSON

Library and Archives of Canada Cataloguing in Publication Data

Thomson, Andrew, 1957-

    Leadership and purpose : a history of Wilfrid Laurier

University / Andrew M. Thomson.

ISBN 978-1-55458-432-1

    1. Wilfrid Laurier University--History. I. Title.

LE3.W48T56 2011   378.713'45   C2011-906609-2

This book has been produced by the editors and designers of the Wilfrid Laurier University Department of Communications, Public Affairs and Marketing, in Waterloo, Ontario, Canada. Additional volunteer layout and design assistance by Kenneth Tam (WLU BA '06, MA '08), an author and publisher, and proud former student of the author.

Photos and images provided by the Wilfrid Laurier University Archives & Special Collections, as well as former university photographer James Hertel, the Laurier Department of Athletics & Recreation, and the Laurier Communications, Public Affairs and Marketing Department.

Marketing and distribution assistance from Wilfrid Laurier University Press
Waterloo, ON N2L 3C5 Canada

Printed in Canada by Thistle Printing Limited, Toronto, Ontario.

"100 years inspiring lives of leadership and purpose."

ACKNOWLEDGEMENTS

As I SET OUT TO WRITE THIS BOOK I knew that I wanted to tell a story, not just recount a list of events. Laurier's past is a rich and fascinating one, and no book could tell all of its stories. As I talked to people and looked through documents it became increasingly clear to me that the story I wanted to tell dealt with the struggle of the school to persevere and even thrive in difficult circumstances. In the end, the message that seemed most resonant to me was the story of an institution facing challenge and building success. This focus has meant that some wonderful stories and many interesting people would not find a place in this book. They live on in the extensive collection of the Wilfrid Laurier University Archives and I encourage you to continue to explore Laurier's history there.

My work on the book was ably assisted by the efforts of Caitlin McWilliams. Caitlin had just completed an MA in history at Laurier when I began this project and she put those skills to work in archival collections at the Kitchener Public Library and the Laurier Archives. In addition to a good eye for historical context, Caitlin brought an appreciation for new digital technology that made my job much easier. Julia Hendry and the staff at the Laurier Archives provided invaluable assistance. In particular, Cindy Preece provided a number of excellent suggestions and had a wonderful memory for both documents and pictures.

The Laurier Archives is an outstanding resource for anyone with an interest in the university and the seminary, and is home to an extensive collection of images. Laurier's office of Communications, Public Affairs and Marketing offered consistent support and encouragement throughout this project. Not the least of this assistance was their arrangement to have Carol Jankowski edit the manuscript. She made that process easy and effective. Kevin Crowley's keen eye and helpful advice were also important in completing the book. Jacqui Tam and Tiffany Bradley were patient, helpful and supportive, although I know I must have complicated their lives endlessly. Most of all I would like to thank my wife, Charmian Christie, for her love and constant support during this project.

I have spent much of my adult life at Laurier, first as a student and later as a contract academic. I still have a great affection for the school and for my many friends within its community. I appreciate very much the opportunity to tell the story of a very special place.

ANDREW M. THOMSON

AUGUST 2011

ABOVE: The Evangelical Lutheran Seminary's official opening and dedication was held on October 30, 1911, on the lawn of the seminary.

INTRODUCTION:
FIVE MEN AND A HOUSE

AMONG THE MANY PHOTOGRAPHS in the Wilfrid Laurier University Archives is one entitled *First Student Body and Faculty*. It shows four serious young men in suits and ties standing with an older man in front of a large house in Waterloo, Ontario. Together they make up the entire student body, full-time faculty and campus of Canada's first Evangelical Lutheran Seminary in 1911, the seminary's first year.

A companion photograph taken at the official opening of the seminary on October 30 of that year—with guests, dignitaries and the curious crowding the grounds and spilling on to the street, the house open and welcoming—has a celebratory mood that contrasts with the rather stark image of the founding class.

However, the serious image may better reflect the institution, reminding the viewer just

how tenuous and isolated the seminary was in its early years. As bold as the experiment was in creating a Canadian seminary for the Lutheran Church, in its infancy the school was very small, focused and by no means secure.

The foresight of the Waterloo Board of Trade in providing land, and the determination of the Lutheran Synod, opened a door to the future for both the community and the church. Both would work hard to ensure this opportunity was not lost. However, in their boldest vision, the small group of pioneers could not have imagined the multi-campus, comprehensive university that would grow from this modest beginning. Despite challenges and adversity, they had laid the foundation that would support tremendous growth to come.

The seminary was vital to the future of the Lutheran Church in Canada. Although well established by the beginning of the 20th century, Canada's Lutherans continued to rely on ministers trained in Europe or in the United States. Consequently, adherents sometimes encountered imposters and, perhaps more seriously, frequent departures from standard Lutheran theology, as well as conflict within congregations.

Kenneth McLaughlin's *Waterloo: An Illustrated History* points to examples of both problems within Waterloo County in the years prior to the establishment of the seminary. St. John's

Lutheran Church, the largest local congregation, lost its minister to a doctrinal dispute with the national church in the 1880s, a schism that lasted more than 20 years. Similar incidents occurred across the country. One goal of the new Waterloo facility would be to create a standard of reliable, well-trained ministers to serve the growing Lutheran community.

Leadership of the Lutheran Church in Canada was divided between the English- and German-language sections of the Evangelical Lutheran Synod of Canada, joined by the smaller Central Canada Synod, which largely represented Ontario congregations. In the summer of 1910, the Evangelical Lutheran Synod's two groups agreed on the need for a seminary, and on the wisdom of appointing a committee to investigate and develop the project. There was also consensus that the University of Toronto was the logical location. U of T was already home to a number of Protestant seminaries and offered access to university courses for prospective students.

The University of Toronto was amenable, and a draft agreement called for the Lutherans to purchase a property on St. George Street in U of T's campus area. They were to be prepared to accept students as early as the fall of 1910.

Such optimism was quickly tempered. Within weeks, at a meeting in Toronto on September 29, 1910, the Lutheran committee learned that the St. George property would cost $24,000, and that the university expected a commitment by January 1, 1911. In addition, the treasurer reported that less than $300 was available for the purchase. Committee members took the January deadline as an opportunity to postpone a decision until year's end. By the time they met again in late December, the treasury had grown to $500, and pastors across the country had been asked to preach in support of fundraising for the seminary. It seemed prudent to ask the university for an extension.

In late March 1911, the committee again met in Toronto. Despite fundraising, the treasury held a disappointing $763. Lutheran negotiators suggested abandoning talks with the university about the St. George Street property. The minutes from that meeting note that "the interest in this motion was heightened by the probable offer of a site in Waterloo or Berlin (later renamed Kitchener) for seminary purposes." The entry was later amended to insert the word "free" before the word "site." Undoubtedly with a sigh of relief, the notion of a seminary in Toronto was shelved.

While the financial implications of a Toronto location were the major constraint, other concerns had arisen. One correspondent with the Lutheran committee worried that with so many other seminaries associated with U of T, "unionistic forms of a common Christianity" would be unavoidable. Doctrinal purity and "Lutheran principles" would be better served in isolation. As well, the committee's German-language group was concerned that their influence would be lost in Toronto's English-speaking sea. It seemed safer to withdraw to the friendlier environs of Waterloo County.

On May 23, 1911, the seminary committee met in Berlin to consider its options. This was a much happier meeting. Rather than seeking concessions, they were being wooed by the Boards of Trade of both Waterloo and Berlin. Board representatives attending the meeting offered free land to facilitate development of a seminary. Berlin had 10 acres of vacant land; Waterloo could provide five acres, upon which stood the Devitt family home — a house that became "a mansion" in Waterloo's presentation. The house would cost $6,500, but the Board of Trade would underwrite that expense on very reasonable terms.

The committee considered and toured both sites. At the end of the day, members postponed any action, but expressed serious interest to both boards. By September, negotiations with Waterloo were concluded, and the Board of Trade provided a down payment of $1,000 for the house. The Synod would pay the mortgage on the house, but the five-acre lot was a donation. A further loan was arranged to expand the land holdings toward King Street and an October 1911 opening was approved. The committee's Dr. Emil Hoffman would serve as temporary president of the new institution. The final note of approval was a letter from the General Council, German Conference of the Lutheran Church, meeting in Johnstown, Pennsylvania, which endorsed the new project as necessary for the future expansion of the Lutheran Church in Ontario and the western provinces.

With the October opening looming, the new institution required faculty and students. Finding qualified and acceptable professors was a significant challenge. Two early selections declined, but the third, Reverend Ottomar Lincke, agreed to become the sole full-time faculty member of the new Lutheran Seminary at a salary of $700 for the first

ABOVE: Postcard of the Lutheran Seminary.

year. Lincke would teach languages and Old and New Testament courses. He would also serve as "House Father" and live at the seminary with his wife. P. G. Hulse of Galt and Robert R. Durst of Guelph were hired as part-time instructors in specialized areas of religious study. Each would be paid $200 for the year.

Then it was time to see if young Canadians shared the Lutheran hierarchy's conviction that a seminary was needed. The initial evidence was positive: a small, quite determined group of young men applied for admission.

Nils Willison, second from the right in the photo of the first students and faculty, was among the first to act. Far from being a typical college student, Willison had quickly risen to become principal of the public school in Coldwater, Ontario, near Orillia. He resigned as principal as soon as reports of the new seminary began to circulate within the Lutheran community. Willison was under contract to the school board and needed its permission to leave. Determined to fulfill what he described as "the ambition of my life, which has been the ministry," Willison asked that they "not only grant my resignation, but realize that as 'we should obey God rather than men,' it is right that I should take this step." The board agreed and Willison and his wife moved to Waterloo. Three other young men,

F. Christensen, Henry Rembe and Medon A. Bitzer, rounded out the first class.

With faculty and students in place, the launch date was set for October 30, 1911. The evening prior, Acting President Hoffman conducted a service at St. John's Lutheran Church where faculty members were installed and Lutheran luminaries spoke. The following day, the official party of local political leaders, members of the Board of Trade and church officials held a ceremony at the new Evangelical Lutheran Seminary of Canada. Before almost 3,000 onlookers, J. Charles Mueller, president of the Board of Trade, presented the deed for the land to the seminary's Board of Governors.

Once the speeches were over and the crowds left for home, the festive atmosphere dissipated. The time for hoping and planning was over. Five men and a house remained to begin the very serious business that lay before them.

ABOVE: Early faculty and students, including
Reverend Ottomar Lincke.

ABOVE: Waterloo College students, 1918-19.

LEADERSHIP AND PURPOSE

CHAPTER ONE
THE FIRST YEARS

I N OCTOBER 2010, signs promoting the following year's centennial appeared around the Wilfrid Laurier University campus in Waterloo. One of those signs featured a phrase that would be prominent in the centennial celebrations: "100 years inspiring lives of leadership and purpose."

This phrase has particular resonance because of the origins of the university. The institution that was born in 1911 on donated property in Waterloo was dedicated to the creation of new leadership for the Lutheran Church in Canada, and both the form and function of the small Lutheran seminary reflected that goal.

However, while it might be tempting to view the school founded in 1911 as a microcosm of the university to come, the curriculum for that first year tells the real story.

In a report to the seminary's Board of Governors at the close of the first school year, Acting President Emil Hoffman itemized each instructor's work. Ottomar Lincke, the only full-time faculty member, focused much of his teaching on languages, with five hours of Hebrew grammar and four hours of Greek grammar per week. In addition, he taught five hours of exegesis of scripture, which is the critical explanation or analysis of Biblical passages. Hoffman also noted that Lincke had assisted his students with "a cursory reading of the book of Concord etc."

Two part-time faculty members also contributed to the curriculum: Professor P. C. Wike taught basic elements of religion and a course in homiletics, while Professor Robert R. Durst taught church history, catechetics and isagogics. The Oxford dictionary defines catechetics as the branch of theology dealing with instruction given to Christians before baptism or confirmation; isagogics is the introductory study, especially of the literary and external history, of the Bible prior to exegesis. Lincke taught in German; Wike and Durst in English.

That was the entire course of study for the first year's students. There were no general arts courses, no literature and no sciences. The new seminary was creating and training leaders for Lutheran ministry and their courses were narrowly focused on that goal.

The curriculum was not the only area shaping students for a career in ministry. Minutes of a 1911 Board of Governors meeting record a set of dormitory regulations and rules of conduct for all seminary students that reflect high expectations, beginning with an outline of how each day should unfold. Students were to rise at six o'clock in the morning, have breakfast at seven and attend Matins at 7:45. The school day began at eight and instruction continued until noon. One half-hour was set aside for dinner or lunch, followed by a period referred to as "intermission." Presumably this was free time until classes began again at 1:30 p.m., continuing until four o'clock. This was followed by two more free hours, then supper from six to seven. In the evening, students were asked to attend Vespers or spend the hour between seven and eight o'clock reading, studying or meditating. After two hours of study, students were to retire at 10 p.m. for the night.

The highly structured day for students living in the dormitory set the tone for the discipline their careers were anticipated to require. In addition to the daily plan, there were rules of conduct to which students were required to adhere. The rules seem almost draconian to a reader in the 21st century, but it is important to remember that students were being prepared for leadership in the church.

There were seven rules:

- *Every student is expected to be a Christian gentleman at all times under all circumstances.*
- *Loud talking or boisterous conduct are to be avoided in the house or upon the street.*
- *Smoking will be regulated in the dormitory and the grounds. It is forbidden upon the streets or*

outside the Institution.

- Students must avoid theatres and places where liquor is sold.

- No serious nor frivolous relations with the opposite sex will be tolerated.

- Students are not expected to be absent from the dormitory after 8 p.m. without permission from the House Father.

- Students are expected to attend Lutheran church services on Sundays, except by permission to the contrary from the House Father.

The first year of seminary records indicate no violation of the rules by the three students residing in the house. Nils Willison lived with his wife near campus.

In his first report to the Board of Governors, Hoffman suggested that while rules were important, it might be best to leave their enforcement to an honour code or to allow students to enforce the rules themselves. While this ideal remained in place, there are certainly indications as time went on that faculty also enforced strict discipline at the seminary.

Hoffman also made no mention of academic difficulties the first year. There are suggestions, however, that some circumstances did challenge the school. From the beginning, former principal Willison played a dual role as student and instructor, receiving a nominal sum to instruct fellow students in areas of general education where they needed help.

The more telling indication of concerns that Hoffman and others had with the quality of the first students lies in his recommendation to the board in the spring of 1912 that the school should accept only collegiate graduates. This implies that some were struggling with the seminary's complex curriculum. Hoffman's goal of matriculated students was logical, but the policy proved impossible to maintain in the early years.

That May, when the board met to consider Hoffman's report, it decided to appropriate the sum of $20 to create a seminary library. Ottomar Lincke, already House Father and the only full-time professor, would be appointed Librarian. Lincke's wife was also kept busy, taking care of both the house and its inhabitants. The workload proved too much for Lincke and he expressed to the board a desire to leave the house and live elsewhere.

Hoffman was agreeable, suggesting a salary of $900 per year and living expenses were

appropriate for a man with Lincke's reputation and responsibilities. The board disagreed, saying Lincke must stay in the house at a salary of $800, which would be an increase of $100 over the first year. As for living expenses, the board agreed to pay for fuel and lights for the seminary building and allowed the Linckes full use of the vegetable garden. In recognition of the couple's heavy workload, the board voted to hire one "Mrs. Franks of Hamilton, Ontario" as stewardess of the facility at a salary of $20 per month. Lincke was to find room for Mrs. Franks in the only building on campus, the former Devitt house (which was located on the site of today's modern seminary at Bricker Avenue and Albert Street).

The following month, the Lutheran Synod met in nearby New Hamburg. The June 3, 1912, edition of the Toronto *Globe* reported that Hoffman told assembled delegates that after a very prosperous year, "the work in the seminary had been greatly blessed" and "the prospect for the future was very encouraging." The first year had challenges, but for the most part they had been overcome. For Hoffman, and the Synod, it was a portent of wonderful things to come.

Enrolment growth was painfully slow, although new students arrived each year. By

1914, the seminary had about 10 students and five faculty. The Devitt house was bursting at the seams and larger quarters would soon be needed.

There was also the issue of improving the quality of incoming students. Hoffman's plan to demand matriculated students proved unsuccessful. Seminary regulations allowed exceptions to the rule, and exceptions proved to be more the norm than anything else. Willison and the faculty were kept busy helping students cope, their responsibilities expanding in an unofficial campaign to achieve the required standards. With effort, the need to elevate students was met, but again progress seemed slow.

Beyond academic challenges, the school faced the problem of feeding and looking after people who lived on campus. In this regard and many others, the seminary turned to the community and Lutheran congregations at large. In 1913, an organization that was to have a profound effect on the future of the school was formed. The new Women's Auxiliary raised money, helped feed students and faculty, and provided emergency support to people in need. Without the auxiliary's great work, the seminary would not have survived its early travails or many of the problems it would face in the future.

A year later, students formed their own group to help on campus. Ministers in Waiting held regular meetings, kept meticulous records and collaborated on raising money and working around campus. They helped build a tennis court, brought in more books for the library and generally aided the school's expansion and development. As usual, Nils Willison took the lead in setting the tone for Ministers in Waiting, serving as its first president.

The year 1914 proved to be memorable for the young seminary. The Toronto *Globe* for June 3 reported that the Evangelical Lutheran Seminary of Canada had its first graduate. Commencement exercises were held at St. John's Lutheran Church, where faculty, seminary students, pastors of the central Synod of Canada English and of Canada Synod German, plus a large congregation, watched Nils W. Willison receive his diploma. Willison became the pastor of a Lutheran congregation in Unionville, Ontario, leaving an impressive legacy as a founding force at the seminary.

Meanwhile, Lincke's burden had been lightened somewhat by the efforts of part-time faculty who were local Lutheran pastors called upon to supplement instruction. However, the careers of the two original part-time professors, Robert Durst and P.C. Wike, illustrate one of the problems with relying on the local pastorate. In 1913, Durst took a better position in Pittsburgh; Wike left for Chicago in 1915. Although both men were replaced by local Lutheran ministers, the turnover meant a lack of continuity in the instruction of seminary students, which remained a challenge for several years.

More significantly for Lincke, a new full-time professor was hired in 1914. Reverend Preston A. Laury arrived from Pennsylvania to teach in English and assume many of Lincke's official duties. Laury was not only named president of the seminary, he was made House Father, allowing Lincke to finally move off campus.

Laury's term as president was important to the school. In his history of the seminary, Oscar Cole-Arnal notes Laury's pragmatic approach to the continuing need for preparatory courses. He separated preparatory courses from official seminary instruction, identifying the special stream as the Waterloo College school, which meant that for the first time non-seminary students could be accepted. This opportunity, and the quality of education, drew some local students to Waterloo College, thereby further integrating the school and the community. While separating the courses was both necessary and beneficial to the survival of the seminary, it also, for the first time, broadened the purpose of the school beyond preparation of clergy.

Laury's second major accomplishment also seemed to be a recognition of the obvious. The original Devitt house could not continue to provide a home for all students, the instructors and their classes. Five bedrooms were set aside for students, and Laury's family, including children, also lived there. They all suffered from overcrowding and a new building specifically built for instruction was clearly needed.

In 1914, a cornerstone for a new teaching building was laid in an old orchard on the property. The Lutheran Church managed to raise $10,000 for the project, which meant the building could be completed on budget and in reasonable time. When it opened in 1916, the building—which would eventually be known affectionately as "Old Main" and later as "Willison Hall"—provided residence rooms for students, a dining hall, a

laboratory for science classes, other teaching facilities and a chapel. The success of the
Lutheran fundraising campaign suggests, among other things, that it was easier to raise
money for an institution that was functioning and providing clergy than for a seminary
that was merely an idea. The achievement is all the more remarkable considering both
fundraising and construction took place during the difficult years of the First World War.

Laury's time in Waterloo corresponded almost exactly to the war years. While his
accomplishments in expanding the seminary and adding the Waterloo College school
were dramatic, his ability to avoid controversy and questions of loyalty during the war
may have been his greatest achievement.

In common with the wider Lutheran Church in Canada, the seminary walked a tightrope
during this period. The background of the faith was clearly German, many churches still
offered preaching in German and much of the instruction at the seminary was in German.
The church and the seminary could expect scrutiny, given that Canada and Britain were
at war with Germany. Under such circumstances, Laury chose to focus on the mission of
the institution, avoid politics and, if possible, keep the school's profile low.

Such caution was not always exhibited by other members of the Lutheran community.

One part-time instructor, Lutheran minister C. R. Tappert, spoke publicly and wrote letters to newspapers about his pride in being German. Many in the non-Lutheran and English communities found Tappert provocative. In an incident underlining the tension and hostility evident in the area, the American-born minister was beaten and driven out of town.

Despite Tappert's association with the seminary, the school did not fall victim to the excesses of rampant loyalists. For much of the war, Laury succeeded in keeping the seminary free of conflict. In fact, as the war continued, more Lutherans began going public with statements and demonstrations of support for the Canadian and British cause. They included Nils Willison, who wrote and spoke publicly about the importance of loyalty and the justice of the Canadian cause.

But while uniformed soldiers participated in services at the seminary, students largely resisted pressure to enlist. Research by local genealogist Brooke Skelton indicates five young men affiliated with the seminary or the college joined the Canadian military during the war, although their dates of enlistment suggest they may have been conscripts rather than volunteers. In any case, none of the five died in the war. During the early 1920s, seminary leaders would point out that fully 25 per cent of the young men associated with the seminary during the war had "done their duty."

In 1918, as the war was winding down, Laury decided to return to the United States. His time as president had been tumultuous, but successful. The new collegiate-level school was drawing students. The new building, already being called "Old Main," was filling up and there was talk of an expansion. The preparatory courses at the seminary were successful and beginning to include first-year university courses.

The future seemed bright at the small college in Waterloo. It was somehow fitting that in 1918, Nils Willison returned to the seminary as principal of the college school. The Toronto *Globe* reported that Willison's congregation gave him a new golf bag as their parting gift, although it was unclear if the dynamic minister would find time for the sport in his new role.

As the 1920s began, the seminary and Waterloo College school were poised for more success. They had survived the challenges of the war years, and enrolments, while still

ABOVE: Reverend Preston A. Laury.

LEADERSHIP AND PURPOSE

low, continued to grow. Support from local Lutherans and the general Canadian Lutheran community was encouraging; the mission envisioned by the founders in 1911 seemed to have come to fruition. And with the college school and new university courses, the beginnings of a broader future were clear.

ABOVE: The 1922 Waterloo College rugby team.

CHAPTER TWO
AN EVOLVING MISSION

A S THE FIRST WORLD WAR CAME TO AN END the small seminary in Waterloo was in the midst of great changes. From its beginning in 1911, the role of the seminary had been clear as an early catalogue for the school put it, "the sole purpose of our institution is to educate and train worthy and competent men in the various branches of theological science, to fit them for the public ministry of the gospel, in the Evangelical Lutheran Church." In 1913, the seminary had been incorporated under provincial legislation. The scope of the school as described in the legislation had exceeded the narrow focus of its founders, as the act of incorporation extended to the institution the right to operate "colleges, schools and seminaries."

The wisdom of this flexibility had become apparent in the seminary's decision to begin

ABOVE: Nils Willison, his wife Margaret, and their daughters Marion, Mildred, Helen and Enid standing on the porch of the Evangelical Lutheran Seminary.

offering high school courses. As the school began to offer undergraduate arts courses, this would become even more significant. By 1923, the new role for the school was reflected in the promotional material they used to attract students. The material included a statement of purpose that showed small but significant changes in the goals of the institution. "It proposes to provide young men well-equipped in mind and heart for activity, and useful in every vocation of life, but especially the Gospel ministry. Being a Canadian institution it seeks to inculcate patriotism and loyalty to this great country and to mould its students into good Canadian citizens." The final sentence clearly reflects the changes and challenges brought about by the First World War; the entire statement reflects a new reality for the school in Waterloo.

The expansion of educational opportunities at the seminary and the school, along with the additional university arts courses being offered, meant that enrolment increased dramatically over the course of the war and the period immediately following it. By the end of the war, 28 students attended classes on the seminary property, a number that would rise as the 1920s dawned. The increase in students and course offerings necessitated an increase in faculty numbers as well. Among the new faculty in this period were professors who would have an enormous influence on the development of the school. In 1917, C. H. Little arrived to teach at the seminary. Little would hold various roles at the institution and teach for more than 30 years, retiring in 1949. In 1918, Nils Willison returned to Waterloo to assume the role of principal at the college school. In 1923, Alex Potter was hired as a professor, becoming dean of Waterloo College a year later. These three men would help shape the nature of the school for decades to come.

As the number of students and faculty rose, one problem that remained consistent was finding adequate funding. The greatest source of funding remained the Lutheran Synods in Canada. The large Evangelical Lutheran Synod of Canada assumed about three-quarters of the institution's expenses while the smaller central Canada Synod assumed much of the rest. Other sources of income included the Nova Scotia Synod which, from about 1920, attempted to raise a sum that would be about equal to the salary of one professor. That said, more money was needed from regular donations from benefactors and special fundraising appeals. For some time after its founding, the school also brought in extra money by renting unused campus property to a farmer. A further source of income was created in 1917 when the General Council of the Lutheran Church in North America formed the United Lutheran Church in America. This body provided both guidance and judgment on policy as well as some level of financial support. One estimate suggested that in the early 1920s the ULCA's Board of Education provided about $2,000 each year to the Waterloo seminary.

Student tuition played a small role in funding the institution. Initially the fees charged to students remained consistent no matter what program they enrolled in; however in the post-war period, the importance of the seminary overcame this egalitarian approach. As more college students, as opposed to seminarians, attended the school, the decision was made to charge tuition fees of $20 for seminarians and $40 for college students. In addition to these fees students were required to pay living expenses and contribute in a small way to the costs of operating the buildings.

Dr. Alex Potter, the first dean of Waterloo College, was born in Berlin, Ontario, in September 1897. After being educated locally, Potter proceeded to Pennsylvania's Gettysburg College, run by the Lutheran Church, where he earned bachelor's and master's degrees in the arts. He later received a doctorate from Columbia University in New York.

Potter was also a veteran of the Canadian forces in the First World War and from his military papers we know he enlisted in 1917 at the age of 20. His occupation was recorded as "student" and he rose to the rank of sergeant before he was demobilized.

Potter arrived in Waterloo to teach in the college school. In short order, he was deeply involved in the process by which Waterloo became a college affiliated with the University of Western Ontario.

Potter taught a variety of courses, including economics and history, and became the first dean of Waterloo College and also its first executive head. In 1928, Potter left, possibly over disagreements about governance, and went to work for Rotary, the service organization. He represented Rotary at a public conference on disarmament in Paris in 1931, and also served as a special observer at sessions of the League of Nations. It's because of that role that Potter became one of the few Canadian holders of the Order of St. Sava, awarded by the Yugoslavian government.

With the onset of the Second World War, Potter returned to Canada and worked for the Department of National War Service in Ottawa. Once the war ended, he returned to Waterloo College as a history professor and also taught courses in economics and political studies. Students found him to be an engaging lecturer whose world travels and breadth of experience made his classes entertaining and informative.

Potter retired from the college in 1954, but returned in 1965 to be awarded an honorary doctorate. In 1954, to help celebrate Kitchener's centennial, Potter wrote a series of columns entitled Let's Reminisce. They were so popular Potter continued them until his death in 1969.

Potter played critical roles at two important points in Waterloo College's development. In the 1920s, he pioneered the liberal arts at the new college and, on his return in the mid-1940s, he helped establish and maintain the institution in an era of intense growth.

As the school became bigger in all facets, it became possible to detect something like a "student life" at the Waterloo property. Much of the recreational aspect of students' lives was organized by groups of students themselves. Willison's "Ministers in Training" program had been a great success and as the school became larger the recreational activities that this group created increased as well. With the introduction of college students the group was divided into seminarians and collegians rather than ministers in training, but the process remained much the same.

One of the holdovers from the Reverend Laury era was the creation of a literary society that sponsored readings and debates often tied to the English-language courses the students received. The German-language equivalent followed suit. An athletic committee was organized, starting with tennis and expanding to include hockey, baseball, rugby, basketball and other activities. There were also amateur theatrical performances and even a quartet based at the seminary.

One student activity that became an ongoing success was the school's Boarding Club, which had been formed in March 1915 and was designed to work co-operatively with all students living in residence working together to collect food and prepare meals for themselves. Lay supporters of the church and, in fact, entire congregations would donate money or food to students who regularly went on drives to the country to collect these food donations. Through these efforts it was possible to keep residence fees to less than $100 per year.

Another benefit of the Boarding Club was the practical relationship between the surrounding community and the school. While the total economic benefit of having the seminary and its ancillary organizations in Waterloo is difficult to assess, and marginal at best in this period, it is clear that the institution ingrained itself in Waterloo and the region in many ways.

LEFT: Waterloo College hockey team.

ABOVE: Fencing on the roof.

RIGHT: Minutes from a faculty meeting asking faculty to remind students not to go onto the roof.

RIGHT: Four students on the roof.

RIGHT: Students playing leapfrog on the roof.

The growth in the size of the school also had an impact on the question of discipline on campus. When the seminary had been one house with a small group of men pursuing a religious mission, good behaviour had been expected and easy to monitor. The idea of student enforcement of an honour code was similarly enhanced by the nature of the early student body. As more students began to attend, and as students not seeking a religious career joined the student body, things were more complicated. Although the records of student honour code decisions no longer exist, records of some discipline matters do survive. Despite the desire to leave enforcement to students, the records of early faculty meetings reveal occasional incidents when the faculty felt compelled to act. These weekly meetings considered a range of internal issues, but on rare occasions breaches of discipline were dealt with. In one case a student had been caught opening mail addressed to other students and faculty members. His explanation that he had been curious about what the letters said obviously did not mollify the faculty. The student was immediately expelled from the school. Some months later the student in question wrote and asked to be readmitted, but the minutes of the meeting noted only that an answer in the negative had been sent. A second case involved a young man named Jack who chafed regularly

Dean's Office, March 15, 1922.

A meeting of the Faculty was held at 4 pm.

The Dean read a communication from the Navy League of Canada inviting our school to take part in educational campaign. The Dean was instructed to offer our coöperation.

It was resolved to forbid students from climbing unnecessarily on the roof of the college building

It was resolved to hold examinations from March 31, 1.30 pm. to April 7. 12. m.

It was resolved to exclude Form I from the oratorical contest, make it optional with Form II and compulsory with Forms III, and IV.

N. Willison
Secy.

ABOVE: Pyramid of students on the roof.

BELOW: Arthur Mehlenbacher working in his residence room.

under the rules of college life. Jack first appeared in the minutes when he disappeared from campus for several days without permission. The school phoned Jack's father, but he had not been home. When he eventually returned to residence Jack was confined to campus for the remainder of the fall term. The punishment did not reform Jack, however. Just two weeks into the winter term he was caught returning to the residence drunk and loud at 3 a.m. on a Wednesday. This proved to be the end of Jack's experience with higher education. These two cases were interesting, but very much the exceptions at the school. Much more typical, if less successful, was a note that appeared in the minutes asking all in attendance to remind students not to go on the roof of the "Old Main" building. Photos from the period show that some youthful exuberance was beyond the control of seminary regulations.

The legislation incorporating the Waterloo seminary had been admirably broad in the scope of activities it permitted the new institution. This allowed the school to offer seminary courses as well as introductory university courses. One thing the legislation did not permit, however, was the granting of degrees, a situation which became more important as more introductory university courses were added to the curriculum. It was unlikely that granting powers would be granted to a small institution, especially one of a religious nature such as the seminary. In the early 1920s, as this problem became apparent, a number of solutions were considered. The small college would need to affiliate with a larger degree-granting institution, but the limited nature of the courses offered and the focus on religion meant that affiliation might prove a challenge.

Concerns about degree granting, as well as the lure of provincial money, proved very accurate when the school approached the Government of Ontario. Premier G. Howard Ferguson was anxious to limit rather than expand the province's role in funding higher education, and he was reluctant to take any action that would expand the influence and reach of the province's major universities. While it might have seemed logical for the seminary to seek some sort of relationship with the University of Toronto, Ferguson was determined to limit the growth of an institution he increasingly found impersonal and overly large. This was accentuated by the premier's view that post-secondary education was not an area that should rely on provincial funds, an opinion that was widely shared among the province's population.

The solution for the school in Waterloo was suggested by the experience of the University of Western Ontario and two small Catholic schools: Assumption College in Windsor and Ursuline College in Chatham. The affiliations of these two small church colleges with Western were approved even though the colleges in question were not in London, Ontario, and despite regulations at Western that stated "no religious test should be required of any student of the University nor any religious observances according to the forms of any denomination or sect." The very liberal interpretation Western placed on this regulation, allowing the Catholic colleges to affiliate with virtually no changes in their curriculum, was an encouraging sign for the Lutherans. In early 1923, President Hoffman and Nils Willison approached Western about the possibility of affiliation between the two institutions. Western declined the suggestion, however, because it was their opinion that too few college-level courses were offered in Waterloo and hence affiliation would be difficult to justify. The Governors of Waterloo College accepted this situation and decided to take action. Alex Potter and Willison were asked to draw up plans for a reorganization that would meet Western's criteria. Waterloo College of Arts was thus established, initially offering the first two years of an arts degree. This plan was approved by the college's board in May 1924. A plan was put in place to offer the third year in 1924-25 and the fourth year in 1925-26.

Potter was sent to negotiate with Western based on the new circumstances, and Western's concerns seem to have been addressed. After a year of discussion the Waterloo Board of Governors met on February 17, 1925, and accepted the terms of affiliation. The next day Western's Board of Governors did the same. In a combination of the old and the new, President Hoffman, in announcing the new status on February 19, requested that all supporting congregations set aside a day of prayer for the future well-being of the school in Waterloo.

The initial faculty had just one full-time professor, Potter, and relied on five part-time faculty borrowed from the seminary, including Willison who also acted as registrar. In September of 1924, as the negotiations with Western proceeded, the new college had an enrolment of 22 full-time students and two part-time attendees. The terms of affiliation

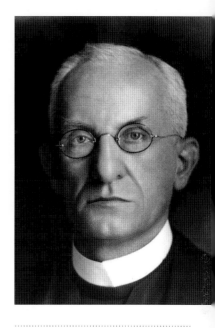

ABOVE: President Emil Hoffman.

ABOVE: Dedication of the "Old Main" Annex.

RIGHT: The Annex dedication program.

granted the faculty status equal to that of their Western counterparts and two Waterloo representatives were appointed to Western's Senate. The seminary's high school section would continue to operate for several years after affiliation but now under the title of Waterloo College School. In 1929 it would be phased out completely.

Following the announcement in 1925, Nils Willison wrote an article in the *Canadian Lutheran* in which he proclaimed, "Lutherans of Eastern Canada practically have a University of their own." This was true, but it was also true that the non-seminary activities of the institution were growing rapidly. As the decade of the 1920s continued, and as the institution entered the darker decade of the 1930s, more change was inevitable.

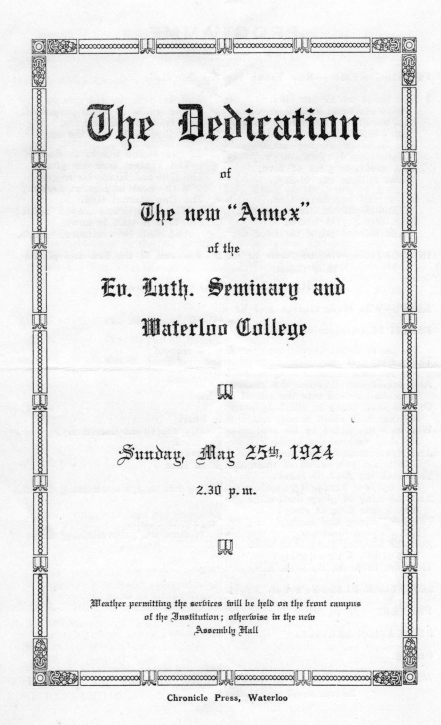

The Dedication

of

The new "Annex"

of the

Ev. Luth. Seminary and Waterloo College

🕮

Sunday, May 25th, 1924

2.30 p.m.

🕮

Weather permitting the services will be held on the front campus of the Institution; otherwise in the new Assembly Hall

Chronicle Press, Waterloo

ABOVE: Boxing in the college gym.

CHAPTER THREE
GROWTH AND CHALLENGES

PRESIDENT EMIL HOFFMAN'S FORMAL ANNOUNCEMENT of affiliation with the University of Western Ontario in February 1925 marked a new era for Waterloo College. The seminary remained at the heart of the institution, but the role of the college was growing and changing. Recruitment of students for the college would become more ecumenical, the curriculum would expand to align with Western's, and more faculty would be required. The new vision meant the school would increasingly struggle to balance the religious and the secular.

The completion in 1924 of an annex to the "Old Main" building improved teaching facilities on the eve of the affiliation with Western. Modern laboratories for science courses, more residence rooms for students and expanded classrooms made the campus more efficient and comfortable. While not yet covered in ivy, the newly expanded brick building increasingly resembled the classic college architecture of the period.

In the early years of affiliation with Western, the curriculum at Waterloo College reflected a traditional liberal arts program, which included introductory courses in mathematics and science. Foundations were being laid for the future of the college, both in the development of courses and enhancement of student life on campus. Enrolment grew as students were drawn to the potential for a university education in the comfortable setting of the college. This was especially attractive to local students in Waterloo, whether Lutheran or not.

By the late 1920s, more than 90 Lutherans and non-Lutherans alike were enrolled, most of them at the college rather than the seminary. However, institutions associated with the seminary continued to play a prominent role. In the 1926-27 school year, 60 of the 93 students were in the student-organized Boarding Club, which arranged the purchase or donation of food for student meals. The Women's Auxiliary expanded its support and fundraising, and the faculty continued to grow, numbering 17 full-time people by 1931.

Numbers would decline during the Depression and the Second World War, but there were sufficient faculty to offer a wide range of arts courses. In the early period, seminary faculty taught at both the college and the seminary, but while 75 per cent of faculty were Lutheran clergy or laymen, non-Lutheran teachers also joined the campus.

One special decision was needed to reflect the school's new circumstances. Prior to affiliation with Western, the school colours were maroon and gold. Would joining the Western family change that? Purple and gold became the colours of choice and remain so to this day. Purple represented the connection to Western, whose colours were purple and white. Gold represented ties to the past. Together they signified the best of tradition and hope for the future.

In writing about his time at Waterloo College, both as student and professor, Carl Klinck recalled the quality of courses in English, Canadian history and his own role as lab assistant in chemistry classes. The foundation of Waterloo's courses must have been strong: the first graduating class in 1927 had six students, including Klinck who was ranked first among Western's class of 1927.

ABOVE: Students playing baseball on the college lawn.

One offshoot of the affiliation with Western was the introduction of Economics 020. The course, initially taught by Alex Potter, was an introduction to political economy, but it was also the beginning of a program that would eventually develop into the School of Business and Economics.

Other features of campus life expanded, too. A new student newspaper, *The Cord,* began to chronicle campus life. In 1928, a group led by the Seagram brothers donated an athletic field as a tribute to their father, which helped an already flourishing program of student athletics. In 1929, the Waterloo College hockey team won the local Lutheran League. The Literary Society from the Laury era evolved into the Athenaeum Society, a group dedicated to cultivating debate and discussion in a forum that encouraged public speaking and, in Willison's words, helped students to acquire "culture."

The many photographs available of Waterloo College and the seminary in this period show a campus of smiling young men in jaunty hats. Collegial spirit is evident in the pages of *The Cord* and in pictures. A 1927 *Cord* editorial, entitled "Our Purpose," said the mandate of the college was "to turn out men of character and gentlemen. Too often our

larger colleges just manufacture doctors, lawyers and engineers."

The paper's goal for the school was admirable, but it implied a further step away from the early statement that "the sole purpose of our institution is to educate and train worthy and competent men in the various branches of theological science, to fit them for the public ministry of the gospel, in the Evangelical Lutheran Church." This divergence would have repercussions at the highest level of the institution.

The growth in faculty and students was accompanied, at least initially, by rapid change at the administrative level. Implementation of Waterloo College's affiliation with Western was Hoffman's last act for the institution to which he gave so much. Hoffman, who was named president in 1920, resigned in the fall of 1925 and died the following April, having lived long enough to see the expanded college's first year of operation.

Hoffman's successor was Austin A. Zinck, the first seminary graduate to become a full-time faculty member, teaching theology and mathematics, and the first to become president. Zinck served for just two years, leaving to assume the ministry of a parish in Milwaukee. The departure for the United States was ironic given Zinck's passion for including Canadian patriotism in the message of the seminary.

Zinck's departure left the president's office unoccupied for some time. The vacancy was a visible symptom of a significant division within the leadership regarding the relationship between the college and the seminary. The expansion of the college, student body and academic programs available in Waterloo had the effect of altering the purpose of the school while increasing expenses. There was also disagreement about the content and conduct of classes.

The division encompassed three of the greatest names in the school's history. Opponents in what was a quiet, yet intense conflict were represented by Alex Potter and Nils Willison on one side and C.H. Little and many seminary faculty on the other.

Potter and Willison believed the administration of all three components of the institution—the seminary, the school and the college—should be under the control of a single administrator or president. Potter nominated Willison. Little disagreed, both with the choice of Willison and the idea of a unified administration. Little thought the seminary and its students were weakened by the association with the college. He hoped to keep the schools separate and argued that seminary students agreed. In letters to his mother, Little complained about Willison's ambition and the threat to the quality of seminary education. Willison's views are available only in the more circumspect official record, but the financial benefits of consolidated administration and Willison's own vision of education were factors. In a move possibly related to the dispute, Potter left the school at the close of the 1928 school year.

When the Board of Governors rejected Willison and Potter's recommendation in the fall of 1927, Willison resigned to become pastor of a congregation in Hamilton. In his letter to the board, Willison attributed his departure not to internal friction, but to a deep conviction that he needed to return to pastoral work. In correspondence with his mother, Little dismissed Willison's decision to leave as a fit of pique at not getting his way.

In April 1928, the board changed its view on a unified administration, in part because of Potter's lobbying, in part because of continuing financial problems. Much to Little's dismay, the board offered the top post to Willison. However, Willison's Hamilton congregation refused to release him from his commitment to them and he was forced to refuse the president's office.

Little's relief, expressed with some enthusiasm to his mother, was short-lived. The board invited Willison to become a governor and shortly after he assumed the board presidency. From this position, he would push for change and closer connections between the seminary and college. Willison noted in his diary that his relationship with Little had "chilled." Little's letters to his mother reveal his strong dislike for Willison and for the new

C. H. LITTLE

Carol Herman Little arrived at Waterloo College in 1917 as a professor of systematic theology, a position he would hold until his retirement in 1947. In the course of his career, Little served as acting president of the college from 1918 to 1920, again from 1929 to 1931, and from 1942 to 1944. He was bursar from 1918 to 1933 and dean from 1920 to 1927.

Little was born in 1872 in Hickory, North Carolina, the son of a Lutheran minister. He was educated at Roanoke College, did post-graduate work at Johns Hopkins University and later attended Mount Airy Seminary in Philadelphia. In 1901, Little arrived in New Germany, Nova Scotia, where he helped create the Nova Scotia Synod and served as both secretary and president of the body.

After an active career in Nova Scotia that saw him serve as both House Father at an orphans' home and the editor of the Nova Scotia Lutheran, Little moved to Ontario. Following three years as a pastor for the Morrisburg-Riverside church, he accepted a call to teach at the Lutheran seminary.

From his position at the Lutheran seminary, Little would bring to bear an intellectual capacity that would have a profound influence not just on the seminary, but on the Lutheran Church in Canada. Little could read six languages and was a prolific writer of books, articles and sermons. He used these talents to reject pan-Protestantism, liberal doctrine and to expound on what he saw as the dangers of female clergy. His was a conservative theology described by his successor at the seminary, Otto Heick, as "typical of the seventeenth century," but Oscar Cole-Arnal notes that this fundamental faith provided the institution with the strength and focus to survive the challenges of war and the Depression.

Little's stern theology was tempered by a personal life filled with family and friends. The warmth of his family life, his theological conservatism and his passion for the institution all left their mark on Waterloo College. For his contemporaries, however, he was perhaps best remembered for his year-round swims in Silver Lake in Waterloo Park.

direction of the school, a direction that became clearer with the next major step in the evolution of Waterloo College.

In March 1929, Willison proposed that Waterloo College begin to admit female students. The board was sympathetic to the idea, raising only one objection related to cost. The concern was considered, but by April the board agreed to open admission to both sexes, appoint a dean of women and renovate facilities at the school to include a lounge for female students. However, because the financial situation precluded a residence for women, enrolment would initially be limited to local females. With these provisos, the board voted to admit female students that fall.

Such a fundamental change occasioned much comment in the community and within the school. It was clear the decision would apply only to the college; the seminary would remain a male bastion. Students and faculty debated the issue informally and in special debates of the Athenaeum Society. According to a study of the debate by Natalie Rubino in a 2007 Waterloo Historical Society publication, the arguments put forward ranged from the danger that females would distract male students and faculty to the potential for increased attendance to improve the school's financial situation. Despite lingering concerns of some in the academic community, the decision was quickly implemented with the hiring of Hannah Marie Haug as the first dean of women.

Haug, who taught history, worked hard to help young women fit into the university framework. Females attended the same classes as their male counterparts, joined campus clubs, wrote for *The Cord* and played sports. The 1929 school year included eight women among the college's 24 full-time students.

The first female student to graduate was Louise Twietmeyer, who had completed two courses at Queen's University, which enabled her to graduate in 1931. Twietmeyer then accepted a teaching position at the college, joining a small but influential group of women faculty that would include Dr. Helen Doherty, who headed the Department of English and French in the early 1930s.

By the end of the 1930s, there were 35 female students. In part due to Haug's efforts, but largely due to the young co-eds' own enthusiasm and ability, women quickly became an important part of Waterloo College life.

ABOVE: Six female students in front of Willison Hall, 1936.

ABOVE: Louise Twietmeyer, the first woman graduate, in 1931.

The possibility that the admission of women would help resolve some of the college's financial problems, despite the cost of preparing to receive them, was just one element in this time of economic uncertainty. In March 1928, Little wrote his mother that local banks were reluctant to accept cheques from the college until some of the debt had been paid back. The governors discussed that issue at the same meetings at which they decided to accept women students.

The board's solution was to appoint a new advisory committee of local luminaries to help the college address its financial needs. The committee was headed by local MP William D. Euler, who was minister of revenue in the Mackenzie King government, and included local leaders such as Norman Schneider, Edward F. Seagram and Charles Greb. Working with Willison, the committee examined the college's needs and options, although the seminary's role, while always present, seems to have been down played.

The committee evolved quickly from sage advisors to fundraisers, launching a two-week campaign to raise money to keep the school open. The target was an ambitious $150,000 which, the committee announced, would pay for the introduction of women to the campus, secure the payroll and allow the expansion of curriculum and facilities to improve science courses. An important part of the campaign, at least as important as bringing in money, was an effort to explain the significance of the college to the community. Kitchener and Waterloo city councils endorsed the campaign, noting the influence of the college on the community. Rych Mills, writing in the annual volume of the Waterloo Historical Society, points out that the focus for both the councils and the local newspapers was the prestige the college brought to the county and the benefit of a local education for the communities' young men and women.

Another theme evident in *The Record* stories and in speeches by committee members was the college's non-denominational nature. Members of faculty and the Board of Governors were also at pains to explain that while the seminary was clearly a Lutheran enterprise, young people of all Christian denominations were welcome at the college. Students were required to attend chapel each day, but the services were designed to be as ecumenical as possible.

As the campaign ended, success was proclaimed. The committee fell short of its $150,000 goal, but achieved a remarkable $112,000 in pledges. *The Cord* headline, "Financial Crisis Has Been Successfully Passed", was optimistic, but the wolf had been chased from the door.

ABOVE: W.D. Euler, who led the fundraising drive of 1929.

Mills' article makes an important point about the timing of the fundraising effort. In the spring of 1929, the community was on the cusp of the Great Depression. Another year or even six months later would have had a catastrophic impact on the campaign. As it was, although $112,000 was pledged, Mills' research shows the amount finally collected was closer to $30,000. Companies and individuals had seen their money swept away by the tide of the Depression and were unable to meet their pledges. Nevertheless, the money raised allowed the board to meet its commitments and to implement the co-educational program.

Fundraising did not stop with the local campaign. Student tuition covered about 40 per cent of the costs of the school and the locally raised funds helped, but the bulk of the funding still came from the Lutheran Synod and other Lutheran organizations. They, like the communities in which they operated, faced major challenges in the 1930s, and the college suffered as a result. In 1935, the college once again appealed to the community for money, although less formally than in 1929.

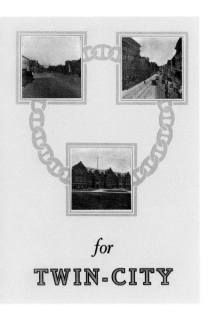

for
TWIN-CITY

....

ABOVE: "For Twin-City" pamphlet from the time of the Euler fundraising campaign.

In a January 1935 interview with *The Record*, Reverend J. Schmieder, Willison's successor as board president, said the school needed $35,000 to meet current expenses, but also pointed out that the school's debt had been reduced and he hoped they might balance the budget for 1936.

 Schmieder also pointed to the largest graduating class in the college's history as evidence of the successful use of their funds. He talked with pride of the small classes and determined students that made the school an educational success. His concluding statement, however, referred to the concern about using public funds in a Lutheran institution. The student body of Waterloo College, he pointed out, was only 50-per cent Lutheran, the rest were from other Christian denominations. He noted that college students did regular university work as part of their affiliation with Western, but "all students also receive religious training, although not with any object of teaching Lutheranism." These last words reflected yet again the evolution from the intent of the early days of the school.

As the board and the community wrestled with the school's financial security, day-to-day business continued. One of the key responsibilities of this period was to select a new president, the first permanent appointment since A. A. Zinck departed in 1928. Frederick B. Clausen was appointed in 1930 and held office until his death in 1942.

Clausen faced many challenges associated with the Depression and the college's slow growth. The new dean of arts, Willis Froats, was to assist Clausen in running the college, but both men would be forced to incorporate fundraising into their daily operations.

In his memoirs, Carl Klinck notes that Froats had high expectations of his teaching staff. Their course loads were heavy and, Klinck points out, their salary did not always increase with their workload. That said, Klinck recalls that he was allowed to teach any subject he chose, and in any manner he thought appropriate, within his field of English.

Klinck's memoirs provide an interesting view of the nature of classes in that period of Waterloo College history. He mentions the range of subjects for the first-, second- and third-year levels and recalls that the small classes associated with the college allowed professors and students the opportunity to explore topics in more depth than might otherwise have been possible. The arts program appeared to thrive, as did business

and economics where Albert Moellman was appointed a full-time instructor in 1937. However, concern lingered about the limited range of science courses available.

Klinck, and Little in letters to his mother, lament the sporadic nature of their paycheques. Both men found it difficult to maintain their family homes while incurring debt with local merchants and wondering when the next cheque would arrive.

Although the campus remained a generally happy place, students in the 1930s shared the financial pressures felt by most Canadians. The Boarding Club was even more important in the Depression years for students struggling to get by. Each year, one student became "Provider," arranging for food, while others helped serve and clean up. During the Depression, many of the usual benefactors of the school were unable to make financial contributions, but local farmers always generously supported students with gifts of food. Sports continued and local church and industrial leagues in hockey and basketball benefited from college participation.

As the 1930s came to a close, the small college and seminary remained in the shadow of their perilous financial situation, but they endured. Froats, Clausen and board members continued to strive for a stable footing, the same battle being fought in many Canadian colleges and homes.

The impact of women on campus had been enormous. By the late 1930s, almost 40 per cent of Waterloo College graduates were female, and women were influential in the faculty and campus clubs. The battle between Little and Willison over a vision for the college and seminary had abated somewhat, partly because Willison left to take control of the Lutheran seminary in Saskatchewan, but the individual identity of each part of the school remained a concern on both sides of the divide.

RIGHT: The members of the College Athenaeum Society in the early 1930s. The society was a social club, a debating society and much more on the small campus.

Norma Maxwell   Jean I. Brent   Richard A.E. Ruch   Audrey D. Froats   Otto F.H. Reble   Carlinda E. Meyers

Rev. H.L. Henkel   Alice M. Siemon   Fred W. Haak   Dr. H. Schorten, Honorary President   Korene Schnarr   Mabel L. Hahn   Elias E. Snider

Ernest T.H. Schroeder   Wilfred W. Bean   Lynden C. Lawson   Carl H. Cooke   Herman S. Scherbarth   Alethea Johnston

GRADUATION CLASS of 1934 from WATERLOO COLLEGE

ABOVE: The graduating class of 1934.

ABOVE: The last peacetime convocation,
held at the University of Western Ontario,
June 7, 1939.

CHAPTER FOUR
A VERY DIFFERENT WAR

T HE CHALLENGES OF THE DEPRESSION were replaced by the onset of the Second World War. Throughout the 1930s, there was growing concern, also reflected at the college, that aggression on the rise within Germany would again plunge Europe, and by extension Canada, into war. The Athenaeum Society regularly discussed the issue and, for the most part, debate in that club and in *The Cord* newspaper suggested Canada should prepare for the worst.

Increased military spending in the second half of the 1930s gradually prepared Canadians for another world war. For some at Waterloo College, the prospect of war might have brought fears that Canadians of German heritage would again face suspicion, as they did in the First World War.

Nevertheless, for the college at least, this would be a substantially different war. Even before war was declared in September 1939, *The Cord* editorialized that "only unthinking and mistakenly patriotic bigots" could possibly associate Lutheranism and, by extension, the college with Germany and the Nazis.

In 1939 and into 1940, the college and seminary's experience was similar to the rest of Canada. At that point it seemed likely that Canada's contribution to the war would be largely economic, with a small military contingent. The federal government suggested that all Canadian universities and colleges should operate as usual, with the proviso that new circumstances might require greater changes later.

Schools like Waterloo College that relied on enrolment for financial stability worried that the war would trigger a drop in attendance. Student numbers were maintained through 1940, but declined by almost 40 per cent in 1941, partly because Waterloo College, like many other schools, eliminated part-time classes. Evening classes were also abandoned and military-oriented activities and training were put in place for most full-time students.

After this initial shock, however, enrolment stabilized and even grew slightly as the war continued. However, at its peak, enrolment in the 1944 school year totalled just 67 students at the college and nine at the seminary. Carl Klinck's memoirs describe one failed attempt by the school to increase revenue while holding the line on expenses. A faculty rebellion that eventually cost Dean Froats his job was sparked by the threat of professors being required to teach summer courses without additional remuneration. Already thin budgets were stretched further and necessary repairs were delayed, but the school struggled on.

For the most part, there was vigorous support on campus for the war effort, although some students recalled arguments in the Library about whether war reparations pushed Germany toward war. Some, especially at the seminary, were appalled by the war's threat to civilization in general. Such hesitation, however, was generally expressed privately. Publicly, the college enthusiastically embraced Canada's role in the war.

The war's most obvious impact on the college was the departure of many young men, both recent graduates and current students, to join the military. More than 120 college

students served during the war, most in the army but some in the air force and navy. Eleven were killed in action. These deaths, and more generally the activities of Waterloo college grads and students in action, were covered regularly by *The Cord* and remained a topic of daily discussion on campus. One graduate in particular, Lloyd Winhold, also a graduate of the Canadian Officer Training Corps (COTC) on campus, rose to great success and was awarded the Distinguished Service Order for bravery in combat.

In contrast to the low profile President Laury espoused in the First World War, President Frederick Clausen organized a committee on military training on campus in the fall of 1940 and an auxiliary reserve began training almost immediately. The initiative quickly evolved into a regular COTC unit at the college. Two faculty members, J. D. Jefferis and Carl Klinck, were deeply involved from the outset, and philosophy Professor James

Originated 20 March 1945

40/P&S/1420 (3080)   C.P.A. 1

9 Can Inf Brigade 3 Can Inf Division 30 British Corps

Schedule No. _____ Unit Nth. N. S. Highrs., C.I.C.
(to be left blank)

Army No. and Rank _____ Major

Name _____ Lloyd Christian WINHOLD (CIC)
(Christian names must be stated)

Date recommendation passed forward	
Received	Passed
Brigade 31 Mar.	1 Apr 45
Division 6 Apr	
Corps 8 APR 1945	5 MAY
Army 7 MAY 1945	4 JUN 1945
4 JUN 1945	

Action for which commended (Date and place of action must be stated)	Recommended by	Honour or Reward	(To be left blank)

On 25 March 1945, when commanding C Company, North Nova Scotia Highlanders, Major Lloyd Christian WINHOLD showed leadership and bravery of a very high order which influenced the capture of BIENEN, Germany, a vital position in the REES bridgehead of the River RHINE.

The village of BIENEN, which had been attacked four times before C Company's attempt, constituted a key to the perimeter of the REES bridgehead. It provided the only exit from the WESTERN part of the bridgehead and was very strongly held.

The initial assault by C Company was made over about 500 yards of open ground. A large number of casualties, including the Platoon Commander and Sergeant of 14 platoon, were sustained from machine gun and mortar fire. Many times, while passing through this devastating fire, Major WINHOLD, with entire disregard for his

Recommended by column:
(D.F. Forbes) Lt.-Col., Comd., NNSH.
DSO

IMMEDIATE
(J M Rockingham) Brig Comd 9 Cdn Inf Bde

(RH Keefler) Maj-Gen GOC 3 Cdn Inf Div

Lieutenant General Commander 30 Corps

Gen.
G.O.C.-in-C. Canadian Army.

P.T.O.

B. L. Montgomery
COMMANDER-IN-CHIEF 21 ARMY GROUP.

Sgd (HDG Crerar) Gen GOC in C First Cdn Army

personal safety, climbed on one of the tanks supporting the attack, in order to direct its fire.

After the first platoon had crossed the open ground, it assaulted a strongly held house by a main road but did not have enough remaining strength to capture it. The Commander and Sergeant of 15 platoon were also wounded. Major WINHOLD personally reorganized the platoon and led the assault successfully through withering fire from the front and both flanks. He immediately proceeded to reorganize his depleted company into two platoons and deployed them.

Major WINHOLD then directed a new attack into the main enemy defences in BIENEN, from an exposed position. Each platoon started on a separate axis, he personally leading one of them. After proceeding some distance the area was counter attacked with three enemy Self-Propelled Guns and a strong body of Infantry. It was getting dark so he moved around in the area of the enemy Self-Propelled Guns forming a firm line onto which he withdrew his leading section, and successfully repulsed the enemy attack. When the reorganization was progressing he again climbed on one of the tanks and directed its fire in the darkness during the whole of the armoured fire fight, in which one of his supporting tanks and one of the enemy Self-Propelled Guns were knocked out. The remaining two enemy tanks then withdrew.

The inspired leadership and great personal bravery exhibited by Major WINHOLD were the means, whereby, this very strong enemy position was cleared for the further operations of 30 British Corps in the WESTERN part of the REES bridgehead. His conduct during the whole six hours of the operation was beyond praise.

If a casualty as under, fill in date.

Nature of Casualty	Date
Killed in action	
Died of Wounds	
Died	
Missing	
Prisoner of War	

RIGHT: Distinguished Service Order (DSO) citation for Lloyd Winhold.

Rickard served as quartermaster for the unit despite the drawback of having only one eye.

COTC recruitment was very successful: 34 students quickly volunteered as cadets, and another 16 enlisted in the military but trained on campus under special programs. Seminary students were exempt, but many volunteered. Students drilled Monday, Wednesday and Friday evenings for at least two hours, took rifle practice at the armoury in Kitchener and trained in other forms of drill on campus.

Although enthusiastic, the early COTC training was found lacking, particularly in proper military atmosphere. The solution, suggested by an inspector sent to look at the program, was to make more extensive use of local militia units such as the Scots Fusiliers of Canada. With their help, the professionalism of the Waterloo contingent increased dramatically.

Originally the contingent was associated with the Ontario Agricultural College contingent in Guelph, but Ottawa suggested that a relationship with the University of Western Ontario, to mirror the affiliation of the college itself, was more appropriate.

While male students trained with the COTC, Professor Margaret McLaren of the History Department, who had replaced former history chair Hannah Haug, organized campus women to work with St. John Ambulance or take Red Cross first-aid courses. Other types of defence training, including map reading and aircraft recognition, also prepared female students for war on the home front.

The military and the COTC were the most formal war-related college activities, but there were also job opportunities for students in war-related industries. A paper presented in a Master of Arts seminar class by Laurier alumnus Barry Ries looks at the lives of several female students who, during the war years, found work at the Sunshine-Waterloo Manufacturing Co. The company originally manufactured agricultural implements, but diversified during the Depression, and in wartime began making metal casings for smoke bombs, fins for aerial bombs and other metal military hardware. Many students and at least two professors found summer employment at the factory, where the work was difficult and the hours long.

Many, including the young women Ries described, struggled with the concept of shift work. Writing in *The Cord* when she returned to school in the fall, one woman

CARL KLINCK

Carl Klinck's story reflects many of the challenges and conflicts that marked the history of Waterloo College. Born in Elmira, north of Waterloo, in 1908, Carl was among the first graduates of the institution after its affiliation with the University of Western Ontario.

At 19, Klinck graduated at the top of his class and departed to work on a Master of Arts degree at Columbia University in New York. Even as he pursued the degree, Klinck was offered the opportunity to teach English at Waterloo College. In addition to teaching, he served as the college's Librarian between 1936 and 1942. Klinck achieved his PhD in 1942 and was promoted to the vacant post of dean of arts at the college. By this time, he had also started an ambitious publishing career, including a book based on his PhD thesis, *Wilfrid Campbell: A Study in Late Provincial Victorianism.*

During the Second World War, Klinck played a prominent role in the Canadian Officer Training Corps at Waterloo College and in his memoir he speaks of his great concern that some on campus who he cryptically identified as Americans, seemed overly sympathetic to Germany. Klinck even recounts a story of uncovering a German spy and reporting him to the RCMP. However, when he took office as dean in 1942, Klinck worked very hard to ingrain what he viewed as a loyal Canadian attitude toward the war and admits he found very little opposition.

In the post-war period, Klinck chafed particularly against the influence of the Lutheran Church on activity at the college. The situation came to a head in 1947 when Klinck resigned, not as he said because he despised Lutheranism, but because too many at the Synod seemed to fail to appreciate the nature of what Klinck called Christian liberal education.

Freed from the constraints of the church-based institution, Klinck continued on an ambitious publishing and teaching program at the University of Western Ontario. The triumph of his career may well be his work as general editor of the *Literary History Of Canada.* In recognition of his enormous contributions to the field, Klinck was made an Officer of the Order of Canada.

recalled encountering Professor Jefferis while she was covered in grease and oil from the production floor. She asked Jefferis how he liked the work, and his response, "Pretty grim, isn't it?" seemed to sum up the factory experience.

However, for the professor and students, a factory wage over the summer was helpful. Jefferis, like many other faculty, was on reduced salary and summer income helped him cope. Other war-related summer jobs were available at the Dominion Tire plant, Canadian National Railway and even raising chickens. Young women volunteered to sew, knit and roll bandages, sometimes on campus but mainly in downtown Kitchener or Waterloo.

One area legislated by the wartime government of Mackenzie King was the role of university students in the conflict. At the outset of the war, the plan was to encourage students to remain in college or university and finish their degrees. However, as the war dragged on, government policy became more interventionist.

Waterloo College was affected in several ways. One government program offering subsidized student loans to people enrolling in science or engineering programs drained students from liberal arts colleges like Waterloo. And as worker shortages became more significant in the later years of the war, the government took a second look at the compulsory service exemption that sheltered students from duty. By early 1944, all universities and colleges were required to report to the National Selective Service Organization the names of any arts students who were in the bottom half of their classes. Whether the students were passing was irrelevant; only commerce and theology students were exempt. The new policy resulted in four Waterloo College students having to drop out and thus become eligible for conscription.

Although the early war years were potentially disastrous to the finances of Waterloo College, the financial situation improved as the war progressed. Enrolment remained somewhat limited, but the general economy of southern Ontario began to boom with wartime production. Economic success locally meant fundraising proposals that had stagnated for some years became viable. Donations from local businesses, bequests and other fundraising in the community picked up dramatically, both for the college and the Lutheran Church, allowing the latter to increase its subsidies to Waterloo College. Records show income from the Canadian Synod of the Lutheran Church rose from slightly over $16,000 in 1939 to more than $26,000 by the end of the war in 1945, and special fundraising campaigns for items such as landscaping were now deemed possible.

While church support was essential, bequests were a significant source of money. In 1944, the estate of Jacob Martin of Waterloo left the college $11,000, and other bequests in the war years totalled more than $10,000.

The rising tide of money meant the college's debt situation began to look manageable for the first time in many years. In the winter of 1943-44, a personal canvass of Twin City industries and businesses by local merchants Claude Musselman and C. N. Weber brought in more than $18,000, eliminating the college's indebtedness.

The United Lutheran College Association, traditionally the college's second-largest donor, not only maintained a steady level of funding through the war, but in 1944 provided an additional $3,000, stipulating that the money be spent on augmenting salaries and library reference works. The happy outcome was that each faculty member received a $100 bonus.

Enthused by the turn of fortune, the college Board of Governors hoped to establish a regular endowment that would be supported by Lutherans across the country. They asked the Synod to establish a committee of pastors and lay people and devise ways of attracting $5,000 in annual donations. The college and the Synod were both disappointed when the fundraising was not as successful as hoped.

At the start of the war, athletic programs were suspended, seemingly for the duration of combat, but gradually they began to reappear on campus, as did some social activities. The college's hockey team competed in the city's industrial league with some success. Women played sports such as badminton, while basketball continued and a men's basketball team also joined city leagues. In 1943, for the first time since 1939, the college held a track and field day.

On the academic front, liberal arts classes continued throughout the war, although with increased demands on faculty. Professor Margaret McLaren was a case in point: hired in 1940, she was expected to teach eight courses a year. When she quite reasonably complained that eight would be impossible, the number was reduced to six, but only because two courses were combined into one and a local high school teacher was engaged to teach the other.

UNTIL THE DAY BREAKS AND THE SHADOWS FLEE AWAY

IN HONOUR OF THOSE OF WATERLOO COLLEGE AND SEMINARY
WHO FELL IN WORLD WAR II
AND OF THOSE WHO DARING TO DIE SURVIVED

FREDERICK C AHRENS	WILLIAM C DUFFUS	DWIGHT E KELLERMAN	LEO R McLAUGHLIN	EARLE C SHELLEY
RUDOLF E AKSIM	J ROSS DUNFORD	ERNEST W KENDALL	GLENN A MacLEOD	GORDON D SIM
OTTO H ALBERTI	GEORGE F DURST	MELVIN A KING	ALLAN K McTAGGART	WILLIAM T SKELTON
CRAIG Mc ALLES	ROBERT V EBY	IVAN M KIRKNESS	MERVYN J NEEB	MAURICE R SMITH
NELSON A ALLES	WOODROW W FOELL	FREDERICK H KLIE	JULIUS S NEFF	FREDERICK H SNYDER
WILLIAM G ARMSTRONG	SYDNEY H FOYER	JOHN E KOEHLER	EDWARD G NEIGH	ANNE E SOMERVILLE
WILLIAM R ARTINDALE	WILLIAM G FRANK	CLARE S KRUSPE	GORDON W C NELSON	ELIZABETH S SPOHN
JOHN D BARTZ	EDGAR A GARTUNG	ELWYN G LEGGE	FREDERICK S OLIVER	JAMES D SPOHN
REUBEN BAETZ	HERBERT W GASTMEIER	WOLFGANG A R LEPPMANN	RUSSELL PARKS	HALVDAN A STRAND
WILFRED W BEAN	HAROLD J GEORGE	WILFRED A LINDSEY	HARRO C R PFEIFFER	A DOUGLAS STUEBING
WILLIAM Mc BEAN	ERNEST F GOMAN	HERMAN L LITTLE	KENNETH W PHELPS	EUGENE P SULISZ
ROSS A BEGGS	WALTER J GOOS	JAMES M LOCHEAD	DANIEL G POWERS	DOROTHY M TAILBY
EARL O BERLE	STUART R GOUDIE	ALBERT A LORCH	F BEVERLEY PUGH	RALPH TAILBY
A FRANKLIN BERSCHT	DOUGLAS H GURTON	DOUGLAS LOWE	MAX V PUTNAM	GRANVILLE TAYLOR-MUNRO
JOHN G BLINKHORN	DOUGLAS W HALLER	E MAEDER	ALFRED E RAYMOND	ROBERT W TEGLER
RUDOLPH A BREITHAUPT	LLOYD G C HALWIG	RUDOLPH C MARTENS	RICHARD O REIBER	CLIFFORD A THOMPSON
ELBERT J BRENNAN	CHARLES F HARDY	WILLIAM J MARTIN	LAURANT A REICHARD	WILLIAM C THURLOW
HOWARD L BROX	JOHN M HARPER	ROBERT D MENZIES	MILTON E REINER	HARRIS C VEITCH
GORDON M BURNS	RICHARD L HARRINGTON	ROLAND A WERNER	WALTER R E REINER	STANLEY S VINCENT
CHARLES D CAMPBELL	ALVIN E HARTMAN	JOHN MILLER	MARK E REITZEL	MELVIN G R WALLACE
JOHN W J CARLISLE	HENRY J HELDMAN	SHERMAN R MILLER	KENNETH J RIPLEY	A ROSS WEICHEL
ALBERT E CARTER	JOHN C HERBERT	WILLIAM B MITCHELL	ROBERT E SAUDER	RICHARD M WELLEIN
MICHAEL J CAVANAGH	LLOYD G HERMAN	VICTOR J MONK	ALLAN P SCHENDEL	C RICHARD WHITNEY
EDWARD G CHADDER	WILLIAM C HILL	FORREST R MOSHER	H E SCHILDROTH	HAROLD A WILLS
CLAUDE A CHISLITT	WILLIAM F G HILLIARD	ARTHUR A MOYER	WILLIAM H SCHLEGEL	HAROLD C WILSON
ROY E D COOKMAN	B HOLM	JAMES C M-CLELLAND	REINHARDT SCHMIDT	ROBERT L WILSON
CARL A CRONMILLER	FERDINAND L HOWALD	HECTOR F McDONALD	JOHN G SCHNARR	LLOYD C WINHOLD
WILLIAM A DETENBECK	JAMES R HUCK	KEITH B MacDONALD	WILLIAM G SCOTT	ROBERT B WOOD
DAVID J DOOLEY	GEORGE INNES	CHARLES D MacINTOSH	DAVID A SHANTZ	VERDEN W YATES
ARTHUR W DOWNE	J NORBERT JEFFERS	KENNETH E MacINTOSH	FREDERICK W SHANTZ	WALTER C B ZIEGLER
			LESTER B SHANTZ	B ZINKANN

PRESENTED TO WATERLOO COLLEGE BY THE UNIVERSITY OF
WESTERN ONTARIO CONTINGENT, CANADIAN OFFICERS TRAINING CORPS

LEFT: The plaque honouring the service of Waterloo College and seminary students and alumni in the Second World War.

Administratively, the college and seminary suffered the loss of President Clausen in 1942. Clausen's tireless efforts to secure the college in the community, and the unrelenting stress brought on by the risk of financial disaster may have contributed to his early death. For almost two years, C. H. Little served as president while the board sought a permanent replacement. They eventually looked south and selected Dr. Helmut T. Lehmann of Wittenburg College in Ohio to guide the school into the post-war period.

Coming as it did at the conclusion of the Great Depression, the Second World War seemed to have the potential to destroy the fragile young college. However, unlike the First World War, this conflict would not see the seminary or college visited by allegations of sympathy with Germany or a lack of patriotic vigour. The initial war years indeed threatened the stability of the school, but as the war progressed the financial situation and the place of the college and its students in the community seemed to become more secure. Ironically, the dark years of war provided the stability that allowed the college and seminary to survive, and when they ended Waterloo College was poised for an even better era.

ABOVE: Faculty member and Dean of Women, Marion Axford, with students in front of Berdux House on Albert Street, circa 1947.

CHAPTER FIVE
POST-WAR YEARS

T HE WORLD BEGAN TO CHANGE FOR Waterloo College even before the end of the Second World War. Especially important was the federal government's program to assist demobilized soldiers with an ambitious benefit program encouraging veterans to seek post-secondary education.

With federal funds directed to potential students rather than institutions, the college avoided the dilemma that provincial money regularly presented. With the decision on where to spend the tuition grant left to individual students, the influx of money was not constrained by Waterloo College's connections to the Lutheran Church. For the first time, a government program meant more money would flow into the college coffers.

The results were almost immediate. Enrolment expanded dramatically, more than

doubling in the first post-war year. Classrooms suddenly filled to overflowing; a new, confident student body had arrived. There was just one troubling trend: the seminary did not share in the growth.

Dr. Helmut T. Lehmann had arrived from Ohio to become president of the college and seminary in the fall of 1944. Barely 30 years old, Lehmann possessed practical and academic experience when he accepted the job. He was the son of a Lutheran pastor and a graduate of the University of Saskatchewan and the Lutheran seminary in Saskatoon, which was headed by Waterloo alumnus Nils Willison. Lehmann was awarded a doctorate in theology from Erlangen University in Germany; his thesis explored church government. A brief pastorate in Winnipeg was followed by a position teaching Greek at Wittenberg College in Springfield, Ohio.

In the first year of his term at Waterloo College, enrolment increased to 172 students from the 66 who were registered in the dying days of the war. Among the new students were 25 veterans taking advantage of the recently created federal grant program. As for the seminary, Lehmann was forced to report to the *Canadian Lutheran* that, for the first time, the seminary had no students to graduate in 1945.

For Lehmann, the institution's problems were complex. With its huge influx of students, the college clearly needed more facilities and faculty. Yet at the seminary, the task was to attract enough students to meet post-war Canada's demand for Lutheran clergy.

Another of the challenges of the post-war period was to improve the college's reputation. Despite its affiliation with the University of Western Ontario and Western's influence on the Waterloo curriculum, the college had developed a reputation as the institution of last resort.

Margaret Armstrong, a student in the late war years and the immediate post-war period, recalled that although there were excellent faculty members, including Carl Klinck and Alex Potter who had returned to Waterloo, there were also weak instructors and "the Library was totally inadequate."

Reg Haney, who arrived on campus in the fall of 1948 for what he describes as a pass arts degree, offers an excellent example of the reason for Waterloo's poor reputation. Haney went to high school in the Hanover area north of Waterloo when, during the war years, students could skip spring exams if they agreed to help Ontario farmers prepare for the growing season. Haney finished high school, but his marks were not the best and he had not written exams in a number of subjects. He left school to work at the local newspaper, but wanted to go to college. The only one that would accept him was Waterloo.

The editor of the local paper suggested to Haney that when he got to Waterloo he should look up Lloyd Schaus, a young man who had previously held Haney's job at the paper. Schaus gave up journalism to become a university instructor, and by 1948 was the dean of arts. Haney arrived at the college and asked if anybody knew a man named Lloyd Schaus. Indicative of the small college's friendly nature, he was immediately ushered into the dean's office. Schaus examined Haney's high school transcript and told him that with such low grades, college rules would preclude admitting him to several of the first-year courses. A downcast Haney cheered up, though, when Schaus decided he would instead admit him to second-year courses in those subjects. It would be Haney's last chance, Schaus said. He must work hard, do well and must write and pass his high school exams when he returned to Hanover the following summer.

Haney, now a Queen's Counsel and long-time solicitor for Waterloo Lutheran University and later Wilfrid Laurier University, recalls that few schools would have given him such an opportunity. Haney made the most of it, moved on to Osgoode Hall and enjoyed a successful career in law. Nevertheless, his experience shed light on how Waterloo College earned a reputation, in some quarters at least, as an institution of last resort.

In the decade following the Second World War, student activity at Waterloo College reflected the vibrancy of the era. The school's athletic teams acquired the name Mules, a play on the name of Western's Mustangs; the women's teams were improbably referred to as Mulettes. The teams met with mixed success, but provided a focus for school spirit.

One impact of the Lutheran connection was a student body with an international flair as students arrived from Africa and across North America. Student activities included the annual Purple and Gold Review, generally an original student musical production. The college choir, led by Dr. Ulrich Leupold, toured parishes of southern Ontario giving concerts. The Boarding Club lived on and, despite the increasing population of the school, the sense of community persisted.

More students meant more faculty were required. The 1946 fall issue of *The Cord* student newspaper reported "no less than four full-time and seven part-time additions to the staff of Waterloo College."

The paper's report on the nature of these appointments, however, also alluded to part of the problem at Waterloo College. Ruth Lazenby, the new instructor in philosophy and psychology, was a gold-medal winner in honours English language and literature, graduating with a Bachelor of Arts degree that same year from Western. Lazenby had only minored in philosophy and psychology, but now found herself teaching those subjects at Waterloo.

Lazenby's associate, Marion Axford, held a Bachelor of Arts degree from McMaster University and had taught mathematics at a high school in Elmira, Ontario, but was appointed registrar and dean of women. John Osborne had a Bachelor of Arts in political economy from McMaster and a wartime career in the Canadian military when he arrived at Waterloo to become a professor of economics and business administration.

Some new faculty were no doubt quite talented, and Axford enjoyed a long career at the college. It is their limited qualifications that strike the modern reader. Small wonder that many new faculty were subjected to the same sort of pranks on arrival that first-year students go through. As *The Cord* noted, "the new faculty members did not escape initiation and to their everlasting credit, we certainly have a wonderful group and such good sports."

Carl Klinck, who became dean of arts during the Second World War, faced a different type of test in 1947. As dean, Klinck reported to the Lutheran Synod annual meeting, and in his memoirs he recalls spelling out the special contribution he felt the college had made to the Lutheran Church by virtue of its success as an institution of liberal education. The Synod representative from the United Lutheran Church organization in the United States interrupted Klinck, saying, "That's not what the Synod wants to hear. Tell them how many of your faculty are communing Lutherans."

Klinck resigned immediately. Although he subsequently enjoyed great success in the English department of the University of Western Ontario, his days at the Lutheran college were over. Klinck's frustration illustrated one of the great tensions that developed in the post-war period: How Lutheran would the college be?

Klinck's departure could not have helped Lehmann's goal of improving the overall quality of the faculty. However, to replace the departing English professor, he hired a woman who would become a legend at Waterloo College, Waterloo Lutheran University and Wilfrid Laurier University.

Flora Roy at that point was completing coursework for her doctorate at the University of Toronto. The department chair at U of T arranged for Roy to meet two gentlemen who had travelled from Waterloo College to speak with her. Lehmann and the new dean of arts, Lloyd Schaus, discussed with Roy the possibility of teaching at the small college in Waterloo, but Roy had her heart set on a position in British Columbia. When that fell through, she reluctantly took the post at Waterloo. "I regarded it as a stopgap that would support me until I finished my thesis and qualified to go on to a *real* university," Roy wrote in a memoir.

As it turned out, she remained associated with the institution in one way or another for the rest of her life. Roy brought fellow University of Toronto graduate Jim Clark with her, and the two made up the college's English Department.

From Roy's memoir we get a glimpse of academic life in the late 1940s at Waterloo College. Roy and other faculty members wore academic robes to lectures, which was

DEAN OF WOMEN

SINGLE ROOM

....
ABOVE: A brochure for Waterloo College's
Residence for Women.

FELLOWSHIP

RECREATION ROOM

RECEPTION ROOM

DOUBLE ROOM

EDUCATION

ABOVE: Flora Roy, professor and chair of the Department of English.

problematic at times: Roy did not have an office at the start, and therefore nowhere to hang her coat or robe. Each fall, the faculty joined colleagues at Western to set curriculum and exams for the coming year. There was some flexibility for the associated colleges, but all honours papers were marked by faculty at Western and exams were approved by the relevant departments there.

About the time Roy joined the faculty, another professor who would have a long and distinguished career arrived. Herman O. J. Overgaard joined the faculty as an assistant professor of economics and business administration, an appointment that doubled the size of the business faculty to two. It also marked the first appointment of a person from the business community rather than from academia or the professions. Overgaard held a Bachelor of Arts from the University of Winnipeg, but it was his expertise in the business world, gained from working for the Cockshutt tractor company in Brantford, Ontario, that attracted Schaus's attention.

For the two men, who became acquainted through Lutheran Church connections, it was the beginning of a long association. It also set up Overgaard, who would later earn a PhD in business from Columbia University, to play a significant role in the development of the college.

Roy's lack of an office was a symbol of the overcrowding that plagued the college in the post-war period. *The Cord* regularly appealed for action. New classrooms, residence rooms and facilities were required, but there was a question of whether expansion would be possible on the existing campus or should they move to a new location. In 1947, President Lehmann urged the Board of Governors to aggressively pursue a new site, pointing out that the restrictive real estate meant the campus could not expand sufficiently for the current student population, let alone for future growth.

That fall, the board discussed the possibility of purchasing the Shantz farm, which held 87 acres of land near Victoria Street in Kitchener. It would allow for new facilities and the potential for growth. Businessman C. N. Weber, a lay member of the board, led this effort and he and Lehmann explained the benefits of the new location to the board, which initially seemed to agree.

Critics of the plan included C. H. Little's son, Fred, a student leader at the seminary.

Little's point was that local connections to Waterloo that had served so well in the past would be lost if the college moved to Kitchener. Others shared his concern, particularly the risk that previous benefactors might be reluctant to follow the college south to the road that led to Guelph.

When the question came before the Lutheran Synod, members accepted the idea of relocation, but cautioned that many within the church were attached to Waterloo and hoped that might be considered. Lehmann's campaign was predicated on the need for new buildings and the Synod suggested a $100,000 fundraising campaign might bring in the money needed to create a new campus at a new location. The campaign to move was helped somewhat by the City of Waterloo's apparent reluctance to provide much of a financial incentive to keep the college in their city.

The debate lasted years. *The Cord* in 1948 and again in 1949 called for quicker action on either expanding or moving. In the fall of 1949, editor-in-chief Helen Taylor published an editorial with the all-caps headline "WHEN ARE WE GOING TO MOVE?" The next year, the paper again raised the issue, saying expansion was impossible until the manner and location were settled.

The delay was based on economics. The $100,000 fundraising campaign had not been successful. Without the college incurring significant debt, money to purchase land and construct buildings was not available. In 1951, the City of Waterloo offered the college three acres of land adjacent to the existing campus and a subsidy of approximately $2,000 to allow the college to begin purchasing more adjoining property from private owners.

In March 1951, the board discussed the issue again. In the end, the option put forward by board member Gerald Hagey, who had chaired a fact-finding committee, was to proceed with development at the present site. The notion of moving to Kitchener's larger location was abandoned and Hagey's plan was approved. C. N. Weber resigned from the board in protest.

By fall 1951, enrolment reached 180 full-time and 36 part-time students. Willison Hall, even with its 1924 annex, could accommodate approximately 100 people. Something had to be done. The old Devitt House—the original building on campus, which had undergone expansion and found many uses in the years since 1911—became the campus's first

THE WOMEN'S AUXILIARY

Many years ago Mrs. Geelhaar Sr. used this recipe for the cake which became her special donation towards the lunch on Visiting Days. This cake had no particular name, but because Mrs. Geelhaar brought one each visiting day, they named it Seminary Cake.

Ingredients:

½ cup butter

1½ cups white sugar

3 eggs (whites beaten & added last)

1 cup milk

3 cups flour

2 teaspoons baking powder

1 teaspoon lemon rind

1 teaspoon vanilla

Bake in moderate oven, in tube pan.

From its inception, the seminary, and later Waterloo College, were male enclaves. Ironically though, the early success and even survival of the school relied on a small, dedicated group of women. In 1913, Mrs. Ida Stahlschmidt launched the Women's Auxiliary for the new seminary. The auxiliary was based on the tradition of the Ladies Aid group that was part of each Lutheran congregation. In her history of the organization, Dorothy Schaefer noted that Stahlschmidt became the first president of the auxiliary. Mrs. Clara Conrad acted as German secretary while Mrs. Martin Beiber was her English counterpart and Mrs. Louise Hagen was treasurer. At first the group was responsible for hosting "Seminary Visiting Day" on the first Saturday of each month when area Lutherans were invited to visit campus. Visitors brought vegetables, blankets or other essentials to help support the little school while the auxiliary served coffee and treats on what the students came to call Cake Day. The hosting duties expanded to helping the students with laundry and cleaning and providing linens and blankets. In 1921, Clara Conrad became the president of the auxiliary. She would hold that office for the next 20 years.

In 1931, the auxiliary asked each church in the Canadian Synod to form a branch auxiliary of the seminary. Each branch would charge a membership fee of one dollar, the resulting money to be sent on to the parent auxiliary. Over the course of the Depression the money raised by the auxiliary was essential in maintaining the infrastructure of the college, and the actions of the women helped maintain the morale of the institution.

Through much of the 1940s a focus for the auxiliary was the apparent need for a women's residence. In 1951, the auxiliary provided not only financial assistance but also furnishings for the new women's residence that was named after Clara Conrad. In addition to this special project the auxiliary continued to raise money for the operation of the college and to provide scholarships as well as lab equipment, furnishings and a plethora of other essentials for the operation of the campus.

Of all the implications that resulted from the departure of the Associate Faculties and the creation of the University of Waterloo, one of the most underappreciated, perhaps, is the increased reliance on fundraising carried out by groups such as the Women's Auxiliary. Schaefer's pamphlet on the history of the auxiliary includes lengthy lists of donations made for scholarships, furnishings and even books for the library that helped the under-funded school survive.

In 1973, when Waterloo Lutheran University became provincially funded, the Women's Auxiliary was faced with a significant choice. At their annual meeting that year a standing vote was taken and the unanimous result was that the Women's Auxiliary would become an auxiliary only to the Waterloo Lutheran Seminary. As the university went forward as a public institution it did so without one of the most important building blocks in its lengthy history. The auxiliary continued, and continues, to play an active role in the vibrant life of Waterloo Lutheran Seminary, but the formal relationship with what had been Waterloo College ended in 1973.

official women's residence, named after Clara Conrad, long-time leader of the Women's Auxiliary. It housed 30 students, which was a beginning, but much more was needed.

In 1952, Lehmann announced that a new teaching and administrative building would be built on campus. Plans included 15 teaching rooms and an amphitheatre, a music room which would also serve as a chapel, laboratories for the sciences and new offices for full-time faculty. The lobby would feature a memorial to the men and women of Waterloo College who had served in the Canadian Armed Forces in the Second World War. A bronze plaque was designed and inscribed, and remains in the entrance foyer of what would become known as the Arts building.

The board also announced plans to construct a dining hall that would accommodate up to 125 students and connect the teaching building to the Clara Conrad residence. The new teaching and administration building would be constructed on land donated by the city, and the overall cost would be just under $500,000. Lehmann estimated construction would begin in spring 1953.

During the 1952-53 school year, students watched the dining hall and kitchen being built. More land was acquired at the corner of Albert and Dearborn streets (now University Avenue), and a cornerstone was laid in September 1953. In fall 1954, students began to use the new Arts building; old Willison Hall classrooms were renovated for use as a library, and former class space and science laboratories were turned into student bedrooms. The physical plant was growing significantly.

The layout of the campus dominated discussion for several years, but at the board level academic questions were also being raised. Change was underway at the college and the seminary. C. H. Little had retired as seminary leader in 1948, replaced by Otto Heick who continued the transition launched by President Lehmann several years earlier.

Although the theology of the seminary could by no means be considered liberal, the extremely conservative nature of the Little years began to relax. Oscar Cole-Arnal's book outlines in more detail the theological changes that took place, but in general a more liberal view of the church began to take hold.

At the college, the strong emphasis on liberal arts was under discussion. The government's post-war education policy seemed to indicate that science and engineering were the important programs. This, in some ways, reflected the government's wartime policies, but in the 1950s, science, mathematics and engineering began to take priority across Canada. It created a challenge for a liberal arts institution such as Waterloo College.

The debate was to have significant implications for the future. Clearly the buildings and faculty of Waterloo College could not offer the sort of courses that seemed to be called for in the new era. How could the college respond?

For some, the new focus was a mistake. In an editorial entitled *"Science… Bah!" The Cord* dismissed the concerns of "protractor friends" and defended the liberal arts. It was a bold statement of principles. Artsmen, as the paper describes them, were society's natural leaders: "The highest esteemed position for which a science man can strive is to be a brilliant servant to his Artsman master," the paper stated.

Student bravado aside, the college faced a serious issue. Science courses would be expensive and the building program that slowly developed in the early 1950s demonstrated that funding from the Lutheran Church was nearing its limit. That limit was not just financial. Even in matters such as the Boarding Club, the question needed to be asked: How large a student body could such a volunteer program sustain? If the school was to grow, new sources of funding and perhaps new kinds of students would be needed.

The college looked to a new president for answers. Lehmann had resigned in the fall of 1953 to work for the Board of Publication of the United Lutheran Church in America. Upon his departure, Ulrich Leupold noted some of Lehmann's career triumphs, acknowledging that Lehmann had not been as successful at fundraising as hoped, but under his leadership student activities had increased, the relationship with the community expanded and enrolment grew by leaps and bounds.

In the search for a replacement, the college for the first time considered the possibility of a president who was not a Lutheran clergyman. The rationale was that a president with connections and experience in business would be better able to generate donations than a cleric. Their choice was lay board member Gerald Hagey, a 1928 graduate of Waterloo College. Hagey had enjoyed success in business, starting as a salesman for B. F. Goodrich Rubber Co. in Kitchener and rising to manage Goodrich advertising and public relations.

Waterloo College was in a difficult position, having been asked by the Lutheran Synod to generate new income to supplement the Lutherans' contribution. In response, Lehmann had arranged to have Kitchener-Waterloo Hospital's nursing students receive some of their training on campus. Hagey experimented with a program he had heard of in the United States, with students conducting rudimentary commercial research for local companies, which then compensated the college.

These were small successes. Hagey also realized the college must gain access to provincial funds if it was to progress. It was equally clear that the province under Premier Leslie Frost would not give public money to a religiously sponsored school.

For inspiration, Hagey looked to Assumption College in Windsor, which had also been affiliated with the University of Western Ontario. Like Waterloo College, it hoped to introduce a science and engineering program and was frustrated both by intransigence from Western about the nature of its programs and by the inability to get provincial money as long as the Catholic Church controlled the institution. The solution was to create a new public institution, which they styled the University of Windsor. Assumption College could affiliate with Windsor, but the university would have a separate board.

Hagey also considered the example of McMaster University in Hamilton, which had been controlled by the Baptist Church until the Second World War when it created a public aspect with a separate board, funded by the province. These two examples of success were important although, as Flora Roy later noted, in each case the church eventually lost control of the institution.

As Hagey explained the idea to the board, it seemed to guarantee success without significant risk. A new body would be created with an entirely public board of directors. It would apply for incorporation for the purposes of offering courses in science, engineering and possibly business administration. Under Ontario law, the new institution would be eligible for provincial grants. The seminary and the college would then affiliate with the new institution, allowing provincial grants to flow to the new campus.[1]

In the spring of 1955, Hagey approached the Lutheran Synod with his plan for what he hoped would be called the Waterloo College of Science and Commerce. When this was established, it would affiliate with the Waterloo College of Arts. Hagey made it clear that

[1] This paragraph attempts to simplify a complex procedure. Kenneth McLaughlin, author of *Waterloo: The Unconventional Founding of an Unconventional University* (University of Waterloo, 1997), offers a detailed and well-written discussion of the permutations necessary to accomplish this step.

without something like this plan, both the college and the seminary faced a bleak future. He said he feared that if the Lutherans did not act, the local St. Jerome's College might, thereby dealing a death blow to Waterloo's hope for expansion and possibly survival.

In the face of Hagey's rather dire predictions, the Synod agreed and a subcommittee was established to work on the project. Hagey's proposed name for the new school was rejected, however, and replaced by Waterloo College Associate Faculties. The new name, the Synod said, would emphasize the central role of the college in future plans. With the approval of the Synod, Hagey moved forward. A new era was in store for Waterloo College.

ABOVE: Male students in dormitory, 1947.

ABOVE: George Becker, vice-president; Gerald Hagey, president; Carl Dare, treasurer.

LEADERSHIP AND PURPOSE

CHAPTER SIX
DIVISION OVER ENGINEERING

T HE FIVE YEARS FOLLOWING THE Lutheran Synod's acceptance of Gerald Hagey's proposal for Associate Faculties was a period of confusion and excitement. Records reveal feelings of hope, betrayal, excitement and resentment. The documents, and even more so interviews conducted at the time and since, show very different understandings of what was being proposed, and varied views on what happened to those proposals. It was a period in which questions and animosity threatened the relationship between the college and the University of Western Ontario, risked tearing apart the college faculty, and left students wondering what would happen to their degrees. Optimism and despair often shared the stage, but the college continued to grow.

Hagey's bold plan to establish a separate institution free of religious sponsorship would require land for new classrooms, a library and residences. The college's small land holding did not have space for the new institution and Hagey wanted the new teaching body, the Associate Faculties, to purchase adjoining land with provincial funds.

Acquiring the land was more difficult than anticipated. Aerial photographs from this period show what appears to be available land, but the owners were reluctant to sell. Hagey's dreams seemed threatened by the constrictions of the small campus, and he tried unsuccessfully to enlist the federal government in an attempt to acquire land controlled by the Central Mortgage and Housing Corp.

Other, perhaps more distant locations would need to be examined. Recalling the great disputes at the beginning of the 1950s over the proposal to move the college to Kitchener, Hagey was reluctant, but circumstance forced his hand.

As Hagey battled for more land, curriculum for the new Associate Faculties was quickly being developed. From the beginning, it was clear the new entity would offer science courses, but Hagey and the advisory board now talked of expanding into engineering. Although it would become controversial, the board and many of its followers were excited by the potential for something special. The situation was complicated by the fact that the University of Western Ontario had recently launched its own engineering program. Western viewed with suspicion the possibility that Waterloo College might offer a competitive program under the auspices of their affiliation.

Hagey and his friend and former B. F. Goodrich associate, Ira Needles, who had joined the board, were enthusiastic about the prospect of a new and special kind of engineering school. Just how special became clear as the idea developed. Hagey, Needles and others on the board began to explore the possibility of a co-operative form of education for engineering students. Under this plan, students would alternate three-month terms of campus classes with similar terms spent working in industry. This would allow students to make some money and employment contacts, while industry benefited by tailoring the expectations of the program to the realities of the manufacturing world.

The plan was innovative in Ontario, although there were precedents at U.S. universities and engineering schools, including Ira Needles' alma mater, Northwestern University in Chicago. Excited about the potential, Hagey and Needles contacted local companies and

ABOVE: Aerial view of campus in 1957.

expanded their research into the American experience with co-op education.

It was also important to inform the Ontario government as quickly as possible about the plan. As they prepared their first grant request for provincial funds for the Associate Faculties, Hagey realized the engineering program was a departure from what had been discussed earlier with the ministry. He worried that this new, relatively untested plan might jeopardize the general success of the application, but found enthusiasm for the idea at Queen's Park. There was even talk of expanding the budget set aside for the project.

Somewhat naïvely, the proponents of what was now being called the Waterloo Plan hoped other Ontario engineering institutions would not be annoyed by the new proposal. Needles, Hagey and others saw their program as a supplement to the existing engineering education community, something new but not a threat.

However, hope that other schools, especially Western, would not object was short-lived. While Western was willing to recognize some science courses for the new school, it was adamant about not recognizing any part of an engineering program.

In the summer of 1956, Hagey, Needles and others on the board pushed forward. Similar programs at U.S. universities were studied. Canadian industries were consulted and they responded with enthusiasm. While much of this background work was still underway, Hagey and Needles made the proposal public in a manner that annoyed Western and other engineering faculties.

One objection from the start had been that the technical nature of the proposed education would undermine the proposal's academic credibility. Significant opposition

CANADIAN OFFICER TRAINING CORPS

In 1940, following Canada's entry into the Second World War, Waterloo College introduced the Canadian Officer Training Corps program, or COTC, which for many young men was their introduction to military life before enlisting in the regular army.

The resident staff officer was Captain Jim Clark, a professor of English who led the young men in a program of general military knowledge. Clark was assisted by Major Ross Virtue of the Queen's Own Rifles, whose responsibility for the University of Western Ontario COTC included regular visits to Waterloo College. Students who wished to join the COTC applied to become officer cadets and could choose from various army roles including infantry, armour, artillery, service ordinance and pay corps. Given the presence of the seminary on campus, the chaplains corps was also a popular choice.

In the post-war period the COTC continued, and by the 1950s it had become a regular part of college life. Waterloo College's yearbook, *The Keystone*, reported that in 1955 the COTC received 12 young officer cadets, the greatest enrolment since its formation.

During the school year, COTC cadets attended lectures and functions at the headquarters of local units. Officer cadets spent part of their summer at Camp Borden in Ontario, undergoing training to turn them into effective soldiers and leaders. The three-month training session tested the mettle of the young men. After completing two phases of COTC training, the students received their official commissions as second lieutenants. The COTC option led to a militia commission, but if a young man chose to pursue a career in the regular army he could enlist in the Regular Officer Training Plan.

For more than 25 years, the COTC was a regular part of Waterloo College and later Waterloo Lutheran University. However, political fashion of the day and declining enrolment resulted in the federal government ending the program.

The author wishes to thank Major Harold Russell whose memories of his experience as a COTC cadet in the 1950s provided much of the information for this article.

coalesced around the idea that Waterloo College was a liberal arts facility lacking extensive scientific courses or any background in engineering or science, and was in any case a small college with a local, not national reputation. How could such an institution develop quickly into one that offered the critical engineering instruction required by a co-op program?

Despite criticism and limited facilities, Waterloo College began the process of launching the Associate Faculties.

By the end of 1956, the ambitious scheme was proceeding rapidly. Hagey had managed to gain approval for the Associate Faculties, except for the engineering issue, to affiliate with the University of Western Ontario. Students who were to attend pre-engineering in co-op courses would not be registered with Western. The division would create complications, but by then it was too late to turn back. In the coming year application forms would be developed, a program outlined and the beginnings of the co-operative program put in place. The new school was developing at a breakneck pace.

At times things seemed to be happening too fast. There were questions about the look of the new institution, its relationship with the seminary and the college, and how the students and faculty would be acquired. Even governance of the new institution was questioned.

As president of Waterloo College, Hagey would also be president of the Associate Faculties. College Dean Lloyd Schaus would also be dean of the Associate Faculties. There would be two separate Boards of Governors, but Hagey hoped his dual position would allow him to control the process as it went forward. And go forward it did. In February 1957, Waterloo College and Waterloo College Associate Faculties agreed to launch the first section of the applied science course that July, although it was still not clear where classes would be held.

On May 31, 1957, Associate Faculties purchased two portable buildings, called Annex 1 and Annex 2, from the Ratz lumber company and installed them behind Willison Hall for Associate Faculties classes. Despite the confusion, external conflict and some indecision, Waterloo College Associate Faculties began successfully in July.

The sudden influx of science and engineering students to the campus was most obvious

in the fall when the arts students returned. Almost immediately there were rivalries. The engineers, who were visibly proud of the importance of their discipline on campus and in Canada, were dismissed as plumbers by the arts students. Most of the friction was light-hearted, but genuine disagreements existed and within a year the Engineering Society withdrew from student government.

Student life thrived as reshaping of the college preoccupied administrators and faculty during the second half of the 1950s. Arts courses that formed the heart of Waterloo College continued and faculty and student numbers increased. *The Cord* reported regularly on student dances and concerts.

Early 1950s student Reg Haney recalled Waterloo students occasionally wandering downtown for a beer at the Waterloo Hotel or another establishment. The legal drinking age at the time was 21, but no one in the community, the college or the Waterloo Hotel was particularly concerned about that. However, that began to change, and in 1958 the Waterloo Hotel informed the college and its students that they would begin to check customers' ages. Arts students blamed the crackdown on the engineers.

Meanwhile, the Waterloo College Mules and Mulettes continued playing, although the Mules struggled on the football field. Toward the end of the decade, after two consecutive seasons without a win, *The Cord* commented that not only were their fans limited, at times members of the squad seemed to lack interest themselves. Practice facilities were limited, too, and finally one angry football player challenged the critics to come out and see if they could do better. It was, in other words, typical campus life, carried on as the institution around them changed almost daily.

The pace of events surrounding the transition from Waterloo College Associate Faculties and Waterloo College to a new institution to be called the University of Waterloo was so rapid and multi-faceted that at times it is difficult to maintain the chronology. At each stage various factions came to different conclusions and presented different interpretations of events.

In the midst of the tumult, several key players developed. Surprisingly, one was Edward Hall, the University of Western Ontario president who strongly disliked Associate Faculties and its plan for a co-operative engineering program. For some time Hall had encouraged faculty members at Waterloo College to consider separating for a return to the days of college and seminary.

Another faction represented faculty who felt a bond with the traditions of Waterloo College and saw Hagey's plans as a threat to the heritage of the Lutheran institution. As time went on, they also felt misled by Hagey about the role the church college would have in the new institution.

The Board of Governors of Waterloo College, while concerned about some developments, remained attached to the program of federation and encouraged the Lutheran Synod not to drop its acceptance of the project.

Assessing the pockets of reluctance, a faction linked to Associate Faculties and hence the new University of Waterloo saw an opportunity to create a separate Faculty of Arts at the university. By doing so, it seemed they would break the understanding that Waterloo College would form the Arts Faculty at the new institution.

Hagey felt buffeted by all these groups. For much of this period he was anxious to have the Lutherans maintain a prominent position within the new university, but he grew increasingly frustrated by the slow pace with which the Board of Governors and college administrators moved toward federation. The tumult accentuated both the lack of understanding and the need for quick responses.

Land became the first divisive issue to be resolved in a way that presaged future problems for Waterloo College. Squeezing all of Hagey's dreams into the small rectangle of land around the college and seminary had long been considered a problem. Hagey had been unable to purchase surrounding land at a reasonable price and while he was reluctant to abandon that hope, other board members at Associate Faculties pushed for a daring solution. A 187-acre farm became available west of the campus. Hagey fought the idea of physically separating his new project from the college, even by a few city blocks, but was eventually forced to accept that circumstances demanded the large land acquisition.

In December 1958, Premier Leslie Frost opened a new Chemistry and Chemical Engineering building, originally planned for the college campus, at the new location. More buildings were under construction, all at the new site and all intended for science and mathematics programs. In his speech, Frost used the term Waterloo "university" rather than "college," foreshadowing developments to come.

As the march toward a new university proceeded, part of the Lutheran Seminary history played a role. Under the original legislation, the seminary did not have degree-granting privileges. That power was acquired in common with the college under the terms of affiliation with Western in a complicated arrangement that allowed the granting of degrees in theology. One concern of Hagey and others was that if a public university was created, the degrees granted by the Lutheran Seminary (and by St. Jerome's College, which would also join a new university) might no longer be valid.

This circumstance and other considerations led Hagey and others to construct the enabling legislation around the creation of the University of Waterloo to also establish degree-granting privileges for Waterloo College and St. Jerome's. On March 5, 1959, royal assent was given to the University of Waterloo Act, the Waterloo Lutheran University Act and the University of St. Jerome's College Act, creating for each the ability to grant degrees. For the first time, Waterloo College, or now Waterloo Lutheran University, would be allowed to grant its own degrees.

Hagey assumed the presidency of the new University of Waterloo, leaving an opening in leadership at Waterloo College. The college appointed Herbert Axford as its new president in the summer of 1959, and Axford and Schaus began negotiating the shift of Waterloo College west to become, they had been assured, the Arts Faculty for the new university.

The pace of change, and the nature of that change, was staggering. In a few years, the Lutheran college had seen the creation of an initially small, associated collection of science courses grow first into an engineering program, then into a large new university. It is no wonder that some in the college and seminary community began to feel their life's work was being swallowed whole by a behemoth.

Negotiations were so slow through 1959 that members of faculty and the board at the University of Waterloo grew inpatient, pressing for an accelerated federation process. At the same time, very quietly, some members of the board and faculty began to make contingency plans if Waterloo College did not provide its Arts Faculty. In fact, opinion began to develop that as a full-service university, UW should have an independent Arts

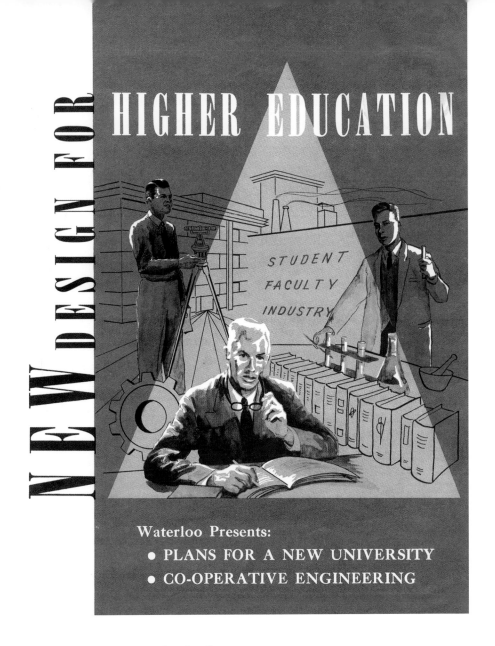

NEW DESIGN FOR

HIGHER EDUCATION

STUDENT
FACULTY
INDUSTRY

Waterloo Presents:
- PLANS FOR A NEW UNIVERSITY
- CO-OPERATIVE ENGINEERING

Faculty not beholden to a church college.

This perspective was accentuated by concerns among some college faculty about academic freedom at the church college. One agnostic English professor was told his contract would not be renewed because he was not a regular communicant of a Protestant faith. Whispers in the halls of both schools spoke of Catholics and Jews who had not been hired at the college for reasons of faith. Some at UW questioned whether a public university Arts Faculty could afford such religious connections.

The Waterloo College negotiators' recalcitrance was hardened by their perception that before the university even opened, their role was being diminished and marginalized. Hagey took pains to convince the Board of Governors of Waterloo College that it was not so, but he also encouraged them to hasten discussion regarding federation. It was becoming evident to Hagey, and eventually he was forced to acknowledge it publicly, that the University of Waterloo might be forced to create its own Arts Faculty.

Both the college board and the Synod had approved the federation plan, with only the specifics to be negotiated. Nevertheless, a small group at Waterloo College actively campaigned against federation. Faculty members such as Herman Overgaard, Fred Little, Flora Roy and others argued that the college stood a better chance of survival if it went its own way. They were somewhat encouraged by comments from Edward Hall at Western, but they also recognized the enormous challenge of preventing what had been presented as a *fait accompli*. To overturn it, the rebel faction would need time and a reversal of the Synod decision.

As 1960 arrived, men like Overgaard and Little travelled to Lutheran parishes across southern Ontario, outlining their concerns that the great Lutheran tradition of Waterloo College was about to be swallowed. They fostered the notion that even if it was difficult and costly, the right and responsible action was to step back from federation and return to the days of a church-based college.

As their campaign progressed, the board, and apparently the Synod, held firm to support for federation and negotiations dragged on. At the end of March, the anti-federation group calling itself the Lutheran Faculty Committee circulated a letter asking for a special meeting of Synod to reconsider. At about the same time, the University of Waterloo decided to develop its own Arts Faculty in the absence of a commitment from Waterloo College. However, as late as April 8, the college Board of Governors met to reaffirm federation. They also took control of negotiations which, until then, had been left to college administrators.

At the University of Waterloo, two parallel arts programs were developing. One assumed that Waterloo College would be the university's Arts Faculty, the other prepared in the event the college involvement fell through. There was a growing sense that a university-sponsored faculty would be beneficial, but Hagey worked to keep that attitude under control.

May 12, 1960, was the critical date. A special meeting of the Lutheran Synod was held in Waterloo where the Lutheran Faculty Committee detailed their argument against federation. They appealed to both the emotional and historical sensibilities of the Lutheran clergy and Synod's lay members. At the last minute, Hagey was invited to respond and did so with some emotion, but no preparation. He was unable to carry the day. At the end of the meeting, the Synod voted to stop the federation process. The college would go it alone.

The reaction was immediate. The college alumni executive met and condemned the actions of the Synod. Several members of the Board of Governors of Waterloo College resigned in protest and 24 faculty members lodged an official complaint. Within two weeks, the president of the college Board of Governors resigned, but to Hagey's bitter disappointment the prospect of federation with the University of Waterloo was over.

So, too, at least officially, was the Waterloo College name. The degree-granting legislation had changed the name of the institution to Waterloo Lutheran University. In the shocked and scrambled days that followed the Synod vote, a new school would be born. It just wouldn't be the one they expected.

ABOVE: Students in the old library of Willison
Hall, 1963.

CHAPTER SEVEN
WATERLOO LUTHERAN UNIVERSITY

IN THE AFTERMATH of the decision of the Lutheran Synod not to federate with the new University of Waterloo, important decisions had to be made quickly. That was not made easier by the atmosphere of surprise, anger, betrayal and confusion that abounded. The resignation of board members, the anger of faculty and confusion about the status of the arts program overwhelmed many involved in the process. Students were confused about where their degree would be issued or whether they would even be eligible for a degree. Faculty members wondered who employed them and administrators began the process of determining what each institution could offer in the coming school year.

It fell to Herbert Axford to resolve the confusion. Axford had been brought to Waterloo to replace Gerald Hagey as president of Waterloo College when Hagey took leadership of the new University of Waterloo.

In his role as president of the college, Axford negotiated with Hagey, represented the board's interests and met regularly with faculty. His background seemed to have prepared him for the position. He had degrees in commerce from the University of Manitoba and the University of Toronto, and a PhD in economics from the University of Wisconsin. After service in the Canadian Navy during the Second World War, Axford had been a professor at Pacific Lutheran University and the University of Alberta.

When Axford was appointed, it appeared his job would be to guide Waterloo College into the role of arts college at the University of Waterloo. However, as the events of early 1960 unfolded, he was in an unexpected situation.

There were other problems for Axford. One long-simmering conflict with faculty regarded the question of whether the traditional concept of tenure would be applied at Waterloo College. It was critical to the college's anticipated role as Arts Faculty at UW, but also relevant if the school proceeded independently.

In the fall of 1959, members of the Faculty Association at Waterloo College had told the Board of Governors and university administrators how they thought tenure and academic freedom should work at the college as it went forward to join the university. On the cusp of the sensational Synod decision, Axford responded, accepting the notion of academic freedom as a good idea, but with concerns. He reminded faculty that Waterloo was a church college, and he noted a number of caveats to the more general claims to academic freedom found in the faculty's initial proposal. He acknowledged that teachers were entitled to freedom in the classroom when discussing their own subject, but he insisted this was "not to be interpreted as liberty to attack or in any way disparage the Christian religion. Teachers are reminded that the college is an agency of the Lutheran Church and is to be used as an opportunity for teachers to bring the light of the divinely inspired truth of the holy Scriptures into the compass of their students."

Further, Axford insisted that controversial subjects not within an instructor's field of study should not be discussed in class. The statement went on to accept the usual implications of tenure in areas such as continuous employment, a probationary term and the conditions under which such tenure might be cancelled.

Axford and Dean Lloyd Schaus did not view the response to the faculty as a negotiation; as Schaus pointed out, they had adopted this position as that of the university. The dean also acknowledged that these conditions of employment might have an influence on the decision of faculty members to stay at or leave the college.

In the aftermath of the Synod decision, this policy became all the more important. College administration knew there was a risk of losing significant faculty members to the new university. To gauge the depth of this problem, Schaus sent a letter to every member of faculty, asking them to make a decision no later than May 27, 1960, and advise him in writing "whether or not you wish to have your contract renewed for the 1960-61 academic year."

One group of faculty wrote the dean on May 26 that they wished to continue their employment at the college on the existing contractual terms, but pointed out in a group letter their decisions should not be construed as approval of the Synod's recent decision not to federate with the University of Waterloo. "Rather," their letter said, "they represent the acknowledgement of our continuing responsibility to Waterloo College students." The next day, however, seven faculty members, including some signatories of the previous day's letter, announced their decision to resign.

Speaking to *The Globe and Mail* in Toronto, Schaus said 20 of 32 full-time faculty members indicated they would return the following year, and he promised appointments were rapidly being made to fill available openings.

One of those new appointments was Loren Calder, a young historian completing the coursework for his PhD in London. As his time in England wound down, Calder was applying for jobs across North America. His application garnered him an offer of employment from Jeffrey Adams, then chair of history at Waterloo College. The offer suggested he would be teaching in the Arts Faculty of the new University of Waterloo, and that faculty would be operated by Waterloo College. Calder and his family booked tickets to return to Canada on June 3, 1960, but on May 28 he received an airmail letter from Adams saying the project with the University of Waterloo was over, Adams himself had resigned, and he did not know what Calder's future might be. When a very concerned Calder arrived back in Canada and sought answers, Dean Schaus told him there was a job in the history department at Waterloo College. Calder spent the rest of his career there.

The creation of two separate and distinct institutions meant everything from office furniture to library books had to be assessed to see where they belonged. Stories abound of typewriters, desks and chairs being taken up the street as college staff struggled to come to terms with the new situation. Into this confusion came a woman whose career at Waterloo Lutheran University and later at Wilfrid Laurier University made her vitally important to the institution's survival.

Tamara Giesbrecht was a young woman with bookkeeping experience at local businesses and the YMCA. When she saw a newspaper ad for a bookkeeper at the new Waterloo Lutheran University, she applied. During her job interview with Axford at his home, the president made it clear he did not particularly agree with the idea of women in business, as Giesbrecht recalled years later during an interview with long-time Librarian Eric Schultz.

Nonetheless, the university's auditor knew of Giesbrecht's work for the YMCA and considered her just the person to whip the office into shape. Harry Greb, treasurer and later chair of the Board of Governors, also had a high opinion of Giesbrecht and she got the job. Within a few days, she discovered most ledgers and other paperwork had disappeared to the new University of Waterloo. Left behind was what she describes as a large box of unpaid bills.

Giesbrecht had little time to consider those setbacks because she had to work on the new institution's first registration of incoming students. All the office staff and most of the faculty worked hard that day to register students. Everyone knew the threshold for success was 500 students, at which point tuition money could keep the school operating. At two o'clock in the afternoon a loud cheer rang out as the 500th student was registered. By the end of the day, 545 students were enrolled.

Giesbrecht faced another challenge as the 1960 Thanksgiving weekend approached. Axford told her the Board of Governors was pressuring him to provide a budget, but it was difficult, given that most of the financial records were at the University of Waterloo. Piecing together scraps of information, Giesbrecht worked at home over the long weekend, diligently pulling together what seemed to her like a viable budget. "It was unique, but it worked," she said later. "There was a lot of guess work." Her process proved to be accurate and successful, and at the end of its first year Waterloo Lutheran had a $33,000 surplus, which grew to $100,000 the following year. They could begin to plan for the future.

Other important decisions needed to be made. The affiliation with Western ended July 1, 1960. One vestige of the relationship was the name given to the athletic teams on campus, the Mules. Now that the teams were no longer poor cousins to Western's Mustangs, a

ABOVE: Winter Carnival program, 1967.

LEADERSHIP AND PURPOSE

new name was in order. An athletics department survey of students generated a number of suggestions, both flippant and thoughtful. "Motherless children" and "Orphans" were dismissed, while "Pioneers," "Royals" and others were seriously considered. In the end, the department chose Hawks for Waterloo Lutheran's teams. Spray paint and glitter on a taxidermy sample of the species resulted in a name change to Golden Hawks.

During this period Waterloo Lutheran students were organizing new and creative activities to enjoy themselves and express their allegiance to their new school. One of the most important innovations was the Winter Carnival launched in 1961. Intended to energize the campus after a long Christmas break, the first Carnival was a tremendous success. Quebec City's Bonhomme de neige made a guest appearance, and the snow sculpture contest, which became one of the enduring traditions, was introduced.

The first Carnival also featured a snow queen contest, a favourite but ultimately controversial event. Designed as a beauty contest including competitors from neighbouring colleges and high schools as well as Waterloo Lutheran, it proved wildly popular, and in 1963 the pageant became the Miss Canadian University Snow Queen Pageant with contestants from across Canada.

As the Winter Carnival grew, the scale of the celebration grew as well. Music concerts, including an appearance by the Supremes, marked what became a five-day affair with the Snow Queen Pageant as the focus. By 1971, however, the sensibilities of the university community and society had changed and the pageant was eliminated. In its place, events such as the popular powder puff football tournament came to the fore. Carnival remains a very popular event on the Laurier calendar to this day.

The enthusiastic spirit of Lutheran students was fuelled by what they perceived as a campaign of pranks against their school by disenchanted former students whom they continued to refer to as plumbers. University of Waterloo students were blamed for a number of incidents of varying seriousness, including the devastating theft of the original Hawks mascot, which was later returned by someone at UW. While hijinks are to be expected between neighbouring universities, the tension around the creation of the University of Waterloo lent these incidents greater significance than they might otherwise have had. In fact, one faculty member from Waterloo Lutheran University wrote the premier of Ontario, asking him to investigate. The premier's office quite logically suggested local police seemed up to the task.

One perception that dogged Waterloo Lutheran was its lingering reputation as "Last Chance U." As Waterloo College did, Waterloo Lutheran University had a liberal admissions policy. Students were accepted with Grade 13 marks as low as 50, compared to schools like the University of Toronto, which required an average of at least 60.

The firm belief at the time, and since, was that while Waterloo Lutheran might have been easy to enter, it was more difficult to graduate there. The low-admission standard did cause problems, though. In some mathematics courses the failure rate was disturbingly high; some science courses yielded similar failure rates as they were introduced. Writing much later, Dean Schaus would note that, in part, the problem was created because the university relied on tuition to meet its financial goals. "I could have set a high admission standard and permitted only the better qualified students to enter, however such a policy

WELF AND OTTO HEICK

When Otto Heick arrived at Waterloo College in 1947 to assume a position as German professor, he launched a family connection to the institution that would last more than 50 years.

Two years after his arrival, Heick switched from the college to the seminary where he took a leading role in teaching theology. Seminary historian Oscar Cole-Arnal viewed Heick's role as pivotal in establishing a new theology, both at the seminary and within the Lutheran clergy in Canada. Over a 60-year career, publishing numerous books and articles defining Lutheran theology and discussing pastoral issues and the history of Christian thought, he helped shape generations of Lutheran clergy. In 1965, Heick was rewarded with an honorary doctorate at a Waterloo Lutheran University convocation.

Heick's influence extended beyond his work with the seminary and the college. His oldest son, Welf Heick, attended the college in the 1950s before completing his degree at the University of Western Ontario. Welf earned a Master of Arts degree at Queen's University and, in 1966, a PhD from Duke University in North Carolina.

Welf returned to Waterloo Lutheran to teach in the History Department and served as its chair for a period of time. He also acted as convocation marshal for 25 years and chair of the convocation committee at Wilfrid Laurier University. Like his father, Welf contributed articles and books in the academic world, including his final book, *Propensity to Protect*, which examined Canada's policies regarding margarine.

Otto Heick was born in Germany before the First World War and emigrated to the United States during the 1920s. Welf Heick was born in Kansas, but accompanied his father to Waterloo in the late 1940s. Taken together, their lengthy careers at the seminary, the college and Wilfrid Laurier University are a testament to the enormous impact one family could have on the history of an institution.

would've created some budget problems." Indeed, each year of the early 1960s saw increased admissions of first-year students.

In the midst of this turmoil, one area emerged as a great success. In the autumn of 1960, Waterloo Lutheran decided to offer a full honours business program instead of just the first two years. Until then, students wishing to complete the four-year program had to transfer to Western, but of course Western was no longer affiliated with Waterloo Lutheran. One area of concern was a university policy allowing admission to any program by any student admitted to the university. This meant the business faculty had to contend with some less-qualified students.

Among the first to be hired for the expanded business program was Glenn Carroll, who would enjoy a long, impressive career as a strong teacher. In January 1962, under Herman Overgaard, the school also introduced an International Business Management program and federal Minister of Trade and Commerce George Hees gave the inaugural lecture. Overgaard had worked with Hees' department to develop the course outline, and the subject matter was designed to stimulate and inform senior executives about business opportunities in international trade.

As the business program expanded, another element of business education began to contract. From 1954 to 1962, the institution offered a three-year program in secretarial science, preparing young women for careers in business. The curriculum was geared to roles seen as appropriate for women with an emphasis on typing, shorthand and traditional secretarial skills. In 1962, Waterloo Lutheran terminated the program and one faculty member, Esther Brandon, transferred to the Business Department as a lecturer. Brandon was the first full-time woman faculty member in business and later served as dean of women and associate dean of students.

The challenges involving Waterloo College Associate Faculties and the events that led to Waterloo Lutheran University had been stressful and hectic, and by the end of the fall term in 1960, President Axford was ready to resign. He left for a career with the federal government, and Waterloo Lutheran began to search for a new president.

The Board of Governors accepted Axford's resignation with regret and, in the first edition of 1961, *The Cord* student newspaper said Axford "filled the breach in the time of crisis, a man who believed in his convictions and took a powerful stand."

While the university temporarily lacked a president, it did have the benefit of its first chancellor, William D. Euler. In the late 1920s, Euler had led a campaign to save the college and was one of the region's most prominent citizens. As a Canadian Senator, president of Economical Mutual Insurance Company and a director of several other companies, his involvement helped ease public acceptance of the new Waterloo Lutheran University. At the university's first convocation, Euler was awarded an honorary degree and installed as chancellor.

Another area of expansion for Waterloo Lutheran was an agreement in 1961 to affiliate with the Mennonite Brethren Bible College in Manitoba. The college, established in 1944, was the national college for the Canadian Conference of the Mennonite Brethren Church, providing theological education and practical training for ministers. From 1961 to 1970, its students could take the first two years of a three-year degree from Waterloo Lutheran while attending the Winnipeg institution, but the Mennonite Brethren then affiliated with the University of Winnipeg and ended the relationship.

One of the connections the Winnipeg college had with Waterloo Lutheran was a teacher named Frank Peters. Peters had graduated with a Bachelor of Divinity from Waterloo College in the mid-1950s, taught for a time at the Mennonite Brethren Bible College and returned to Waterloo Lutheran in 1965 to serve as a professor and later as president.

WLU's new president, William Villaume, arrived in Waterloo in June 1961 to find, as he described later, poor faculty morale and other issues needing resolution. Among the first of the challenges, even before Villaume was installed as president, was the University of Waterloo's decision to end the co-operative arrangement in which it taught science to Waterloo Lutheran students. To hold on to the students, Villaume had to quickly create new science courses.

Then, a short time later, Senator Euler died, forcing the new university to begin another search for a chancellor. As vice-chancellor, Villaume assumed the duties temporarily.

Villaume had arrived at Waterloo Lutheran with his own agenda for change. Tamara Giesbrecht remembers "he had a plan to develop the college into an exclusive residential Lutheran college and, really, that was not the sort of student body we had." Villaume's

ABOVE: William Villaume and future premier William Davis.

ambition for a small, elite school seemed to fit the pattern that was suggested when Waterloo Lutheran split from the University of Waterloo, but the nature of the student body made that difficult. Quite apart from the students, there was debate about whether the faculty, physical plant and library could satisfy Villaume's ambitions.

Villaume recalled that he worked hard to restore faculty morale. Among his successes in that regard was the 1962 creation of a university Senate. The Senate included department chairs and dealt with most day-to-day academic questions rather than forwarding them to the Board of Governors.

His presidency lasted six tumultuous years. During that time, 16 buildings were constructed on campus in the most successful, ambitious building campaign in the institution's history. The challenge of paying for them was met in a new way. Research by Herman Overgaard and others suggested student residences would be eligible for Central Mortgage and Housing Corp. (CMHC) loans at low interest rates. The university's contribution would be land, which was already available. In addition, a Canada Council grant eased the expense of constructing a theatre auditorium.

So successful was the use of CMHC money to construct residences that they were built at the expense of teaching facilities. In 1961, the first section of the new Clara Conrad

Waterloo Lutheran mortgage bonds sale agreement.

Hall for women was opened. The 1962 list was even more impressive: a dining hall, a Student Union building, the Theatre Auditorium and a men's residence known as West Hall. In 1963, a new seminary building was completed along with the East Hall men's residence, a new wing on the Arts building and an addition to the women's residence.

The pace of construction was astonishing. Within two years, the first two floors of the current library had been completed, and in 1969, after Villaume's departure, the five-storey teaching building opened. The campus had almost literally sprung up.

Some classroom facilities remained a challenge and there was disappointment that old Willison Hall had to be taken down, but a plan to upgrade it had been abandoned because the structure wouldn't permit renovation.

Despite its ability to borrow money from the federal government, Waterloo Lutheran required careful, conservative spending to survive. One-time bookkeeper Giesbrecht, who was promoted to vice-president of finance in 1967, noted that during the 1960s, although grants came initially from the federal government and eventually also from the province, they only amounted to two-thirds of the revenue other schools received.

Nevertheless, Waterloo Lutheran operated in the black each year, partly because faculty were required to teach 25 per cent more classes than faculty at other schools.

However, the real key to Waterloo Lutheran's healthy financial picture was its extension program. "Summer school and extension were the gravy train of the Lutheran days," Giesbrecht said bluntly. The only cost was the stipend paid to instructors, while the university received grants and tuition for an entirely new crop of students. The timing was perfect: the Ontario government decided to require elementary school teachers to have a bachelor's degree when previously they had only needed a teaching certificate. The government would help teachers achieve the extra qualifications while Waterloo Lutheran's extension program and bustling summer school provided the courses.

The university was not shy about requiring faculty to participate. Loren Calder recalls being required to teach summer and extension courses as a condition of employment. He received a stipend for the additional teaching, but no academic credit and the work interfered with his attempt to complete his dissertation. That said, the revenue from extension and summer school kept them all employed.

By 1963, Waterloo Lutheran offered extension courses in Kitchener, Waterloo, Guelph, Orangeville, Orillia and Walkerton. Three-hour classes were held every second Saturday beginning each September and running for 14 weeks. Topics included history, philosophy, psychology, economics, business, mathematics and other disciplines.

Student numbers demonstrate the importance of extension and summer courses to the university. For the 1965-66 academic year, Registrar Henry H. Dueck reported enrolment of 5,583 students, including 2,262 in regular classes, 14 in graduate studies, 47 at the seminary, 1,635 at summer school and 1,400 in extension classes. Another 70 were nursing students from Kitchener-Waterloo Hospital and 155 were at the affiliated Mennonite Brethren Bible College. Summer and extension enrolment exceeded the full-time undergraduate component, which was not unusual.

Villaume's term also saw the on-campus course offering expand significantly. By the fall of 1966, the business and economics program at Waterloo Lutheran University was the third-largest in the province. It was time for a separate department. In March 1966, Herman Overgaard had proposed the establishment of a School of Business and

Economics, and the Board of Governors approved the concept the following month. The board also wanted a director to head the school, and Overgaard became its first director.

The new school embarked on an aggressive program of hiring and expanded course offerings and within four years the number of business professors had doubled to eight, plus a seventh economics professor. Prominent names in the history of Waterloo Lutheran, including John Weir and Ralph Blackmore, were both hired in this period.

In January 1967, Glenn Carroll succeeded Overgaard as the director of the School of Business and Economics. One of the lasting innovations of the Carroll years was a high school stock market game, which had its roots in Blackmore's in-class stock market simulation. The success of this project led the school to sponsor an extensive high-school competition in partnership with the Toronto Stock Exchange, which is still going strong more than 40 years later.

One area that needed to expand was science, although that growth would be gradual. In the first year at Waterloo Lutheran, some arts students who needed science electives to graduate were forced to take courses at the new University of Waterloo, but when Waterloo balked at cross-registering students on an ongoing basis, Waterloo Lutheran moved quickly to establish its own courses.

Arthur Read, who later became dean of arts and science, and then the first dean at Laurier's Brantford campus, remembers his recruitment prior to the 1966 school year. Ray Koenig, who was head of science, visited McMaster University where Read was completing a Master of Science in physics. After watching Read in a tutorial, Koenig invited him to visit Waterloo Lutheran University. Read candidly admits he had been anticipating a career as a high school teacher, but the opportunity to work at a university was tempting.

After a follow-up chat with Koenig in Waterloo, he met Dean Lloyd Schaus and finally was ushered in to see William Villaume. By the time he left the president's office he had been hired.

At the time, Waterloo Lutheran offered a three-year general degree in science, but first-year classes of 60 to 70 students shrank to five or six students by third year. Read noted the program was small and there didn't seem to be any intention of expanding it.

ABOVE: Students in the old library of Willison Hall, 1963.

The university's first Bachelor of Science degree had been granted just one year earlier to Margaret Ann Elash. Her convocation also marked WLU's 1,000th degree following the granting of privileges in 1959.

Even in the Waterloo College days, the institution was involved in music education. The seminary offered church music programs for many years, and music courses had made their way into the general arts curriculum. In 1969, Waterloo Lutheran introduced a three-year Bachelor of Music degree although students still had the option of a general Bachelor of Arts with a music major. The Bachelor of Music program remained within the Arts Faculty, and students were encouraged to develop perspective through courses in related areas.

One of Villaume's more dramatic moves was the launch of a graduate program in social work. Villaume had a background in the field in the United States, as did his assistant, Arlette Pederson, and he saw an opportunity to create something prestigious. On the 25th anniversary of the Social Work Faculty, Professor Shankar A. Yelaja wrote a celebration of the faculty's success in which he notes that Villaume reasoned "there was a need for the school and it did not require new infrastructure."

The Senate had adopted Villaume's proposal for a Master of Social Work program in

January 1963. He and Pederson worked hard on it, meeting with federal and provincial governments, professional associations and local administrators to make sure the proposed faculty would be successful. Three years later, in March 1966, Sheldon Rahn, who Villaume met through the National Council of Churches in New York, become the first dean-elect and the Faculty of Social Work's only faculty member.

From his office on the second floor of the seminary building, Rahn began to construct a curriculum with the assistance of Villaume, Pederson and four senior University of Toronto faculty who lent their expertise to get the program running. Classes began in September 1966. The first professor hired was Francis J. Turner, editor of *The Social Worker* and a man with extensive experience in Catholic social work organizations. The first class had 28 men and women. Early on, the seminary and the new Social Work Faculty joined forces to offer a joint master's degree program. Even Villaume's critics were forced to admit the Faculty of Social Work was one of his great victories.

The master's-level Social Work Faculty followed master's programs in several other disciplines, the first of which was romance languages. The hiring of Dr. Neale H. Tayler as chair of Waterloo Lutheran's Department of Romance Languages paved the way for expanded offerings and, in 1964, a French House was established in a two-storey house at the south end of the campus. Furnished in the French style, with French cooking, newspapers and periodicals, Tayler thought the immersion experience would help students project themselves into another culture.

That same year, Villaume announced that the first Master of Arts degree program would begin in the fall of 1965 in romance languages. Tayler was also named chair of the new Council of Graduate Studies in Arts on campus, and consideration of other graduate programs began. Several more would be launched before Villaume's term as president ended.

In addition to the rapidly expanding academic menu, Waterloo Lutheran athletics grew with the renaissance of the Golden Hawks football and basketball teams. When the university was created in 1960, its football team and others competed in a tier of the Ontario Intercollegiate Athletic Association with Osgoode Hall and Ryerson Polytechnical Institute. But WLU Athletic Director Dick Buendorf and football coach Bob Celeri had considerable success with the football Golden Hawks and in 1963 they moved to a higher level of competition with teams from McMaster, the University of Ottawa and Royal Military College. Members of the football team and their coach valued versatility and athleticism, typified by noted alumnus Paul Heinbecker. Heinbecker's success on the field would be paralleled by his later success as a Canadian diplomat and in academics, and he remains involved with the university to this day.

The turning point for the university's athletics programs was the appointment of a director of student activities. In September 1963, Fred Nichols arrived with a Master of Science degree from West Virginia University. Nichols got involved in every facet of university life and remains active in its development even today. In terms of athletics, Nichols' most significant role may have been his influence in bringing a fraternity brother from Fairmont College in West Virginia, David "Tuffy" Knight, to Waterloo as the new athletic director in 1965.

The news release about the appointment noted that, in 1964, Knight had been named football coach of the year in southeastern Ohio, and that for six years he had been a senior high school athletic coach and teacher, coaching football, basketball and track and field. Knight's success was almost immediate. Beginning in 1966, the men's basketball team won seven straight provincial championships, first under coach Knight and later under Don Smith, his successor as basketball coach who arrived in 1970.

The football team also saw continued success. After moving to a higher competitive tier, Waterloo Lutheran continued to play well. In 1966, Knight's first year as coach, the team advanced to the College Football Bowl game, where the Golden Hawks, undefeated in Ontario, met the also undefeated St. Francis Xavier Axmen from Nova Scotia. The game, played at Varsity Stadium in Toronto, did not go the Hawks' way and they lost 40-14. Nevertheless, football at Waterloo Lutheran had developed a national reputation.

Despite the apparent success of the Villaume years, there were problems, some of them revolving around his personality. Hard-working, intense and focused, Villaume expected a great deal from his administration. In his campaign to turn Waterloo Lutheran into an elite school, he often stepped on toes. Lloyd Schaus, the long-serving dean of arts, later complained that Villaume isolated him from most of the significant decision-making, yet held him accountable if problems arose.

Administrators and even some members of the board found Villaume's preference for working late into the night and his lack of patience with criticism difficult to handle. Tamara Giesbrecht, appointed comptroller and business manager in 1963, reflected on the important role played by Villaume's assistant, Arlette Pederson, who acted, in Giesbrecht's words, as a buffer between him and the staff, faculty and administration. Former student leader Bill Ballard recalls that Villaume was something of an enigma to students.

As the 1960s proceeded, Giesbrecht kept the university in a surplus each year, but only at the expense of additional workload for faculty and by limiting other facets of university life. Facing internal division and the ever-present threat of financial stress, the university hired consultants in 1967 to consider its direction. As Booz, Allen and Hamilton Co. examined administration, faculty and curriculum, rumours about the consultants' findings began to circulate.

Campus reaction, particularly at the administrative level, was significant. In June 1967,

Villaume announced that he intended to step down immediately, explaining that the board should be free of commitments at the senior level so it could take full advantage of the recommendations anticipated from Booz, Allen and Hamilton. Arlette Pederson also resigned. Less than two weeks later, Lloyd Schaus resigned as dean of arts.

At the time, the resignation was explained as a decision by Schaus to take advantage of a sabbatical offer, but a letter to board Chair Harry Greb indicated that Schaus was being forced out as part of a housecleaning associated with the impending consultants' report.

When the report was issued, its findings created a stir. One of the most significant recommendations was that Waterloo Lutheran University should abandon its fledgling graduate program to focus instead on undergraduate arts and humanities. The consultants also argued that the new Bachelor of Science program was a mistake, and that science instruction should be restricted to courses required for the Bachelor of Arts program.

The consultants argued that the university's strengths in liberal arts were apparent, and that field offered the best opportunity to help students achieve personal development and academic success. "It is also clear that from a financial point of view the Liberal Arts concentration provides the most likely chance for Waterloo Lutheran University to

ABOVE: In the fall term of 1950, Waterloo College students borrowed a 600-year-old tradition from Oxford University. The Boar's Head dinner (pictured here in 1963) originally celebrated the victory of an Oxford student who used only a philosophy textbook to dispatch a wild boar. His fellow students held a banquet in his honour and that celebration was adopted by Waterloo College students to mark the end of first term. Every year since then, students have gathered to watch the procession of the boar's head, and enjoy a feast of turkey and other delicacies as fall-term classes end.

ABOVE: Boar's Head Dinner, 1963.

achieve higher levels of academic excellence within the limits of the resources available to it," the report said.

Campus reaction was immediate. Not surprisingly, science students and faculty rejected the findings and argued for preservation of their program.

The consultants had also recommended retaining and perhaps strengthening the business program, a position supported by faculty and the broader university community.

While the report generally may have slowed the development of the graduate program, it did not destroy it. The consultants' strongest influence was at the administrative level, where the departure of Villaume and Schaus was simply the first step in reorganization at the top.

Villaume was replaced temporarily by Henry Endress, who had been hired to help with fundraising but had risen to become vice-president and director of university resources. Giesbrecht went from business manager and comptroller to vice-president of finance, the first woman in Canada to achieve that office. Psychology Professor Frank Peters was named dean of arts and science and elevated to the new post of vice-president academic, while Dean of Students Dr. Fredericks Speckeen was promoted to vice-president of educational services.

In response to the first preliminary report from the consultants, the Board of Governors issued a statement reaffirming the status of Waterloo Lutheran as "an independent, private-enterprise university related to the Eastern Canada Synod of the Lutheran Church in America." The board remained convinced the university could continue operating as an economic and financial success within the existing limits of funding. The board noted that voluntary support from industry, the church and individual citizens, as well as Ontario's willingness to allocate at least partial grants to the institution, permitted "a continuing role as a university that strives to serve the developing student and scholar in a unique way of academic life."

With Endress as acting president, the board launched an intensive search for Villaume's replacement. The search gradually concentrated on Frank Peters, who was an intriguing choice. He was a Mennonite, not a Lutheran, and therefore a radical departure from school tradition. He was well respected as an academic and as an administrator, but his appointment suggested that the school's direction might change.

One area Peters influenced was relations with student leaders. Under Peters, Student Union President Bill Ballard was consulted regularly and appointed to Senate and administration committees. In Ballard's opinion, that was only appropriate since the Student Union had, in his words, "its own treasury" and had donated $100,000 to expand the Library. Fred Nichols says that while there were student protests about university governance during that period, they were mitigated by the degree to which student leaders already played a role.

Once he accepted his appointment as president, Peters discovered he and the school faced enormous challenges. The days of capital grants for buildings had come to an end, yet expenses continued to rise. Faculty began to discuss amongst themselves, informally at first and later more officially, whether the time had come to seek provincial recognition.

Looking back on this period, lawyer Reg Haney recalls that whenever he represented Waterloo Lutheran before a provincial legislative committee in Toronto, the question inevitably arose as to why Waterloo had two universities. The implication was clear: many in the legislature thought Waterloo Lutheran should be absorbed by its larger neighbour.

However, a small but significant group within WLU was determined to maintain the association with the Lutheran Church and remain independent of the province. Hence, the statement following the Booz, Allen and Hamilton report that the board and the administration were dedicated to such independence.

Across campus, however, that determination was fading. Historian Loren Calder recalls wondering each year how much longer Waterloo Lutheran could survive, and Tamara Giesbrecht remembers the opinion she attributed to Peters that "if the university was to continue, it needed to have funding or we could not compete for the better students."

Peters decided to push for provincial funding. In January 1969, the Board of Governors passed a motion that Waterloo Lutheran should seek to become a provincially funded university. Peters subsequently asked then Education Minister William Davis, who later became premier, under what circumstances the university might qualify for full public funding. In 1972, Peters told the Lutheran Synod about the discussions. The Synod was not able to significantly increase its spending on the institution, and Peters and the board suggested Waterloo Lutheran be allowed to seek provincial status, under a new name, as a secular university.

Conditions set by the province remained consistent throughout Waterloo Lutheran's existence. To qualify for full public funding, the current Board of Governors had to be replaced by a non-denominational board more fully representing the community. Also, the word Lutheran had to be replaced in the name. As was noted at the time, merely dropping "Lutheran" would have left the name Waterloo University, which inevitably would cause confusion with the University of Waterloo.

The Synod seemed sympathetic, but there were obstacles. Some faculty at both the seminary and the university still cherished the long-time relationship with the church. Today's seminary principal-dean and registrar, David Pfrimmer, recalls that on both sides thoughtful people of goodwill felt their position was necessary and of long-term benefit to students. That did not mean, however, that the debate was easy or unemotional.

In 1972, the Synod provisionally accepted the idea of a shift to a public institution, but there were issues to negotiate. One of the most telling was compensation to the Lutheran Synod for its years of investment in the college and later the university. The provincial cabinet was firm: there could be no question of "purchasing" the institution.

However, the Lutherans were not prepared to walk away from the land, buildings and management value that Waterloo Lutheran held. The emotional matter almost threatened

ABOVE: A meeting in the Torque Room.

to derail the process.

The solution, when it came, was developed by Giesbrecht and endorsed by Peters and the university's negotiators. Giesbrecht suggested they fix a sum of approximately $3.5 million as compensation. Rather than ask the province to pay, they would use their own operating funds. A Phillip Street property owned but not used by the university would be turned over to the Synod to sweeten the deal. In a meeting lasting less than one hour, the province agreed the university could take out a bank loan to pay the Lutheran Church more than $3 million, and at that point the process of provincialization could proceed. The seminary building and the land on which it sat were excluded from the deal.

For two months, Giesbrecht and Peters visited Lutheran congregations to explain the agreement and answer questions Giesbrecht later described as "loaded." Some congregations and faculty members continued to disagree, but when the Synod met later in 1973 the transition was approved by a vote of 212 to 56. It would be official in November, and on the appointed date the Synod treasurer went to Giesbrecht's office. She suspected he was pessimistic about receiving the funds, but she had a certified cheque ready in the amount of $3.5 million. The funds were on loan from the Canadian Imperial

Bank of Commerce, and with effort the loan was paid off by the following summer.

The transfer of funds and closing of the deal marked the end of the Lutheran Church's role in operating the university, although it would retain ties as a federated college. After 62 years, what had begun as a small seminary dedicated to the instruction of future Canadian Lutheran clergy had grown into a new, public institution. The incredible effort that the Lutheran community in Canada expended to keep the school vibrant meant Ontario inherited a thriving institution of higher learning as a page turned in the history of the institution that would now be called Wilfrid Laurier University.

ABOVE: Residents of Willison Hall, 1963-64.

ABOVE: Then-Justice Minister Jean Chrétien
visits campus, 1980.

CHAPTER EIGHT
IN THE PUBLIC EYE

ACCORDING TO LEGISLATION passed by the Government of Ontario, the official date upon which WLU began to stand for Wilfrid Laurier University was November 1, 1973. At a special fall convocation, the new charter was presented and, as can be seen in photographs now hanging in the Senate and Board Chamber, a sign reading Waterloo Lutheran University was turned over to reveal Wilfrid Laurier University on the other side. History Professor Richard Fuke, who had just joined the university, remembers sitting at his first convocation, hoping someone had remembered that when they turned the sign over, the writing would need to be upside down. He was relieved to find that had been taken into account.

Provincial status would launch a new era in the university's history. Access to the full entitlement of public funding meant more money to hire new professors, carry out planned building projects and expand facilities. Programs which might have been in danger seemed more secure and thoughts turned to making the transition as smooth as possible.

Among administrative matters, Frank Peters, the last president of Waterloo Lutheran University, offered his resignation to the new Board of Governors of Wilfrid Laurier University. He thought it was important that the board have a clean slate going forward. The board, however, encouraged Peters to remain as president and he agreed to serve one term.

Recalling those days, Fred Nichols, now dean of students emeritus, remembers students took the changes in stride. Classes continued and campus life seemed very much the same. One thing that did not change for some years was the daily chapel service, a tradition dating back to 1911. By the late 1950s, attendance was no longer mandatory, but some students and faculty found the mid-morning break was an opportunity for both caffeine and reflection before classes resumed.

Bill Ballard, who attended classes in the late 1960s and early 1970s, recalls no pressure to attend. Students were required to take a course in religious studies, but Ballard enjoyed the course enough to take others on the topic. The chapel tradition persisted on the schedule for several years. Classes would start at 8 or 9 a.m., with the break at ten o'clock. Eventually the start time was standardized to 8:30 a.m. and the tradition ended.

The move to public status allowed the university building campaign to continue, and even before the legislation creating Wilfrid Laurier University was approved, two floors had been added to the library building.

As public status came into effect, a new Student Union building sprang to life. Nichols recalls the rationale of first building facilities they knew would be most needed, and in the Student Union building that meant a large, potentially licensed area to provide a meeting place for many groups on campus. Over the course of the next few years, the rest of the building was completed.

Also on the cusp of provincialization, the new Athletic Complex with a 50-metre pool, basketball court, dressing rooms and other sports facilities opened in its current location.

The story behind its construction includes Ballard, who as Student Union president heard that a new fine arts centre would be built first. He inquired why it would take priority over the Athletic Complex and was told the university had received a donation dedicated to a fine arts facility. Ballard's response was that the Student Union would personally match that amount if the Athletic Complex could be built first. A student vote overwhelmingly endorsed it and the new, expansive facility was completed just as Laurier came into being. When the Athletics Department moved into its new home, its former space in the Theatre Auditorium building accommodated the expanding Music Department, staging of plays and other uses.

As the university prepared for its new life in the public sector, it looked back to recognize many who had contributed to the development and success of the institution, renaming residences to honour those individuals. West Hall was renamed Ross Macdonald House after the second chancellor and lieutenant-governor of the province. East Hall honoured Nils Willison, the first graduate of the seminary and a man who played a prominent role in the maturing of the institution. South Hall was renamed C. H. Little House, recognizing the influence of a man who had played a definitive role at the seminary. Two graduate residences were renamed to recognize William D. Euler and Ulrich Leupold, and the women's residence became Clara Conrad Hall in a return to the concept of honouring one of the founders of the Women's Auxiliary, which had helped the school survive in the early years.

There were also several significant developments on the academic side. As of May 1, 1975, the rapidly growing Music Department at Wilfrid Laurier was elevated to the status of a faculty. This meant the new Faculty of Music would have its own dean, and a four-year honours music degree would be established. Students could pursue music history and literature, theory and composition, organ and church music, and performance. A general Bachelor of Arts with a music major remained an option for students, and the university anticipated more opportunity for extension and summer session students to complete such a degree.

The first dean of music was Dr. Christine Mather, formerly director of graduate studies in musicology at the University of Victoria. Her arrival supplemented a department

ABOVE: Former Vice-President of Finance, Tamara Giesbrecht receives an honorary degree, 1981.

that already had many strengths. Arthur Read, who would become the dean of arts and science, notes the credibility brought to the existing program by men such as vocal music professor and conductor Victor Martens and composer Barrie Cabena who laid the groundwork for its introduction as a faculty. Read himself developed a course in acoustics, which he taught for 25 years. The new Music Faculty expanded an area already perceived as one of Laurier's strengths.

Another traditional area with a good reputation at both Waterloo Lutheran and the new Laurier was the School of Business and Economics. In their history of the School of Business and Economics, John McCutcheon and Robert Ellis comment on the significance of the years immediately following provincialization. Under the improved funding, it became "an implicit university policy to increase the size of the undergraduate business program and other (School of Business and Economics) offerings."

This new outlook coincided with the introduction of Max Stewart as the new dean of the School of Business and Economics. Stewart had taught at Waterloo College during the 1950s and early 1960s, and returned from his position as an economist at the University of Alberta to take leadership of the faculty. Stewart was dean from 1974-75 to 1981-82, a critical stretch of rapid growth during which the faculty more than doubled from 24 teachers to 61.

In 1975, after intense discussion, the university announced that the School of Business and Economics would introduce a co-operative education program. In many ways the program was similar to one Gerald Hagey had introduced to the Waterloo College Associate Faculties in the 1950s, an irony not lost on some older members of faculty. The co-op option, as it came to be known, was the first to be introduced in a business school anywhere in Ontario. Students opting for the co-op program alternated academic terms with practical work terms. They would take the same courses as four-year honours students, but graduate one term later.

The school hired a full-time co-ordinator to assist in finding suitable co-op work placements while the dean outlined the benefits to students, including experience and assistance in financing their education. There was also evidence that co-op graduates in other jurisdictions tended to earn higher starting salaries, and Stewart believed co-op students were more likely to make good career decisions. "Our job is to educate managers for industry," Stewart said. "For many students the co-operative method will be the most rewarding."

Potential employers of co-op students also stood to benefit, Stewart said, because businesses sometimes found new graduates did not suit their needs as precisely as they hoped. Employing co-op students might address this problem. Professor Robert Quinn, who was responsible for overseeing the co-op option, anticipated an enthusiastic response and he was not disappointed.

A year later, the School of Business and Economics introduced a Master of Business Administration program designed to be taken on a part-time basis with evening lectures so executives could earn an advanced degree in four years while continuing to work full-time. The director of the program was Dr. Basil Healy, a veteran professor. In the first year, more than 50 businessmen and women enrolled, with executives from local companies such as Mutual Life Assurance, Borg Textiles and even the comptroller of the University of Waterloo filling the roster.

The combination of new programs and aggressive acquisition of new faculty reflected Stewart and the business school's desire and determination to satisfy Laurier's need to increase enrolment, particularly in its elite offerings. Stewart also continued the policy of his predecessor, John Jenkins, in expanding the business school's research capacity.

Glenn Carroll arrived at Waterloo College in 1951, when he enrolled in the arts program. Two years later, Carroll left to work at General Motors, but he found education difficult to leave behind and re-enrolled at the college.

In 1957, he completed a Bachelor of Arts degree, followed by a Master of Business Administration at the University of Western Ontario in 1959. After a short stint working at Electrohome, Dean Lloyd Schaus convinced Carroll to return to what had become Waterloo Lutheran University.

Carroll and Herman Overgaard made up the full-time business faculty, although the department was expanding quickly. Carroll was a gifted communicator,

having won The Toastmasters International public speaking event in 1960, the first Canadian to do so. Carroll eventually became dean of the School of Business and Economics at Waterloo Lutheran and played a prominent role in the expansion of that enterprise.

Carroll also played a major role in university administration as dean and director as well as serving on Senate and the Board of Governors, but it was his classroom presence for which most remember him fondly. On his retirement in 1995, colleagues in the School of Business created the Glenn Carroll Teaching Fellowship as a tribute to his long career and his inspiration as a teacher.

GLENN CARROLL

One of the terms for provincial approval of Waterloo Lutheran University becoming a public university was removing the word Lutheran from its name. However, keeping just Waterloo University as the name would be confusing, given the proximity of the well-established University of Waterloo a few blocks away on the same street.

So, while critical negotiations continued, a second decision was needed and in 1972 the Board of Governors set up a special committee to examine possible names. With representation from the board, the administration, alumni, faculty, students, staff and the community, the committee considered the options.

The preliminary list had 96 suggested names. Kitchener MPP James Breithaupt represented the board chair, Pastor Robert Binhammer, at the initial meeting of the committee, and Breithaupt's thoughtful donation to the Laurier Archives of much of the paperwork surrounding the process makes it possible to examine how the decision was reached.

After wading through the long list of contenders, the committee decided a subcommittee was required to reduce the list to a manageable number. That subcommittee had three members: Waterloo Mayor Donovan Meston, staff representative Barry Lyon and Professor Jerry Hall. When they met, they categorized the list by famous personalities, historic events, historical groups, place names, regional names and names making use of the WLU initials. Some criteria were established easily. If the institution was to be named after a famous person, the person should be a well-known Canadian, although not necessarily associated with the academic institution. The committee agreed to consider living and deceased Canadians.

When they considered the historical events category, they agreed the event should have occurred near or in Waterloo Region. Similarly, any historical group should be tied closely to the region in the historical record and examples in this category included Mohawk and Iroquois. Place names, similarly, should reflect the university locale, while regional names might encompass Central Ontario or South Central Ontario. Finally, if the initials WLU were to be selected, the committee thought it was important that the name fall

within one of the previously listed categories and fit within its guidelines.

To ensure the list reflected the widest possible range of interest, ads were taken out in local newspapers and in *The Cord*. The President's Office issued a widely distributed memo and alumni were notified of the need for a new name.

From the distance of time, a number of names are intriguing. Variations of Wilfrid Laurier's name appeared on all lists, but other names held potential, such as Adam Beck, founder of Ontario Hydro, and Frederick Banting, a discoverer of insulin. The suggestion of Hagey University must have raised eyebrows on the committee, given Gerald Hagey's role in founding the University of Waterloo, while names with local connections included Conestoga-Grand University, the University of Kitchener-Waterloo, Westmount University, Cambridge University and others.

There were also nominations linked to the institution's past, including Nils Willison, Alex Potter, William D. Euler, and the second man to serve as chancellor, Ross MacDonald.

It is also worthy of notice that through most of the selection process, the committee and others made a mistake that would become familiar to many staff, alumni and faculty: the spelling of Laurier's first name as Wilfred rather than Wilfrid.

The list was narrowed fairly quickly, although names such as Cambridge, which played on the recent move toward regional government in that community, and Ross MacDonald were received with some sympathy.

The final list had seven names. An alumni poll conducted in November 1972 generated clear results: Wilfrid Laurier was the most popular choice among the 1,065 ballots returned (6,000 ballots were distributed, indicating a participation rate of less than 20 per cent). Of the returned ballots, almost 500 made Wilfrid Laurier their first choice. Grand Valley was a close second, followed by Central Ontario and Willison. Upper Canada University, Kitchener University and Mackenzie King University also received significant consideration.

A student poll at the same time also reflected strong support for Wilfrid Laurier. However, one group that

why
wlu*
is
changing
to
wlu**

* Waterloo Luthern University
** Wilfrid Laurier University

included Sean Conway, who would later become a provincial cabinet minister, wrote a letter condemning the selection of Wilfrid Laurier as a gimmick, given its play on the initials WLU.

When the final choice was made, the committee revealed some reasoning behind the decision. Mackenzie King was viewed as too political despite his regional connection, and names like Southern Ontario or even Upper Canada were seen as geographically ambiguous. In the end, Wilfrid Laurier was their wholehearted recommendation.

It is revealing that although Laurier's knighthood was included in the early ballots, the final decision was to omit "Sir." Explaining the choice, the committee did not shy from the notion that the initials played a role in their decision. In the pamphlet they distributed later, they went to some lengths to describe Laurier's successful political career, noting his role as a bridge between the two solitudes in Canada and his quote that the 20th century would belong to Canada.

However, they concluded by noting:

"It is not altogether coincidental that the initials WLU will remain for the new name. Many people have for years referred to the university as simply WLU and the initials have authority in academic circles across Canada. They are also well-known by athletic enthusiasts for the WLU Golden Hawk athletic teams that have earned respect across the nation, having qualified for four national finals in recent years. The initials will provide a link with the fondly remembered years of Waterloo Lutheran University and the exciting, eagerly anticipated years ahead as WILFRID LAURIER UNIVERSITY."

After significant discussion and voting, the name was accepted and in 1973, the Government of Ontario introduced Bill 178 entitled *An Act Respecting Wilfrid Laurier University.*

In arts, Laurier continued to build on earlier strengths. The Archaeology Department offered students the possibility of learning in the Middle East, at Greek and Roman sites in Europe, and increasingly in Ontario. Many more students experienced "hands-on" archaeology close to home. For example, Dr. Norman Wagner led the excavation site discovered on a farm in Waterloo County that proved to be the location of a pre-Columbian native village. In 1975, Louise Ann Fox completed Laurier's first honours degree in archaeology.

The expanding Library and additional resources for faculty meant liberal arts continued to be a focus. The Geography Department adapted the School of Business and Economic's co-op program and department Chair Alfred Hecht anticipated many graduates would step into ready-made jobs with firms that employed them during work terms. The arts co-op program would not match the success of business co-ops, but it did broaden career opportunities for some students.

While growth and expansion seemed to be the order of the day in arts, music and business, science courses were not seen as a development priority. Even after provincial status was achieved, the continued dominance of the University of Waterloo in science meant Laurier's science program was of secondary concern.

The shift to public status did not diminish the importance of an increasing student body to maintain the flow of funds into the university. The 1974 statistics were encouraging in that respect: an increase of more than 100 students put enrolment above 2,400 full-time students. Business and economics contributed the largest part of the growth, bringing in 75 more students.

There was some concern about the decline in part-time students taking courses in the summer and by extension. The university attributed it to a switch by some students to full-time enrolment and also fewer grade-school teachers working toward a degree. In 1975, the university created an Office of Summer Session and Extension Education and although registration had levelled since the amazing growth of the late 1960s and early '70s, total part-time enrolment exceeded 3,000 students, compared to 2,400 full-time undergraduates. A full-time director was deemed necessary to efficiently operate the office and Fred Little was appointed to the position.

In 1976, Waterloo Lutheran alumnus Arthur Stephen was appointed to a new post as director of the liaison office, geared toward increasing applications to the university. Stephen's first year was marked by great success when the percentage of applicants naming Laurier as their first choice doubled. For the fall of 1978, more than 3,200 applicants chose Laurier as their first, second or third choice, an increase of 36 per cent— the largest percentage growth of any Ontario university. President Frank Peters noted with satisfaction that the increase in applications was across the board in arts, music and science, not simply in business and economics.

In 1978, Stephen celebrated with the production of a film entitled *I Chose Laurier* to help promote the university at high school liaison sessions, and on television during half-time shows at college football and other games. Just over 11 minutes long, the film featured a former student who urged potential students to look around before choosing a university, and described Laurier's campus life, course options, residences and sports activities. Well received wherever it was shown, the film won a silver medal at the 21st annual International Film and Television Festival in New York.

In the late 1920s and again during the Second World War, dedicated fundraising campaigns within the business communities of Kitchener and Waterloo helped alleviate critical debt situations at Waterloo College. At other times, the institution relied on donations and bequests to keep the doors open. While some might have hoped that the move to provincial public status in 1973 would alleviate the necessity for such campaigns, it quickly became apparent that government funding alone could not maintain the quality of education the university wanted to provide. It was equally clear that *ad hoc* fundraising campaigns would not be sufficient in the modern era.

Under the leadership of successive presidents Frank Peters, Neale Tayler and John Weir, a new regimen of fundraising was gradually developed. One of the most compelling examples of this new philosophy was the creation in March 1981 of a program called *Excellence in the '80s*, a five-year plan intended to raise $6.2 million from private sources. The university consulted Rowing and Associates of Toronto, which provided ample evidence that a private campaign was not only necessary, but potentially very successful. Premier William G. Davis and his wife, along with Chancellor John Black Aird, agreed

to be the major patrons. A wide variety of Canadian business leaders also agreed to participate.

The campaign not only targeted Canadian corporations, it also drew support from the student body, faculty and alumni. The success of this dedicated campaign emphasized the importance of aggressive fundraising to the future of the institution. Increasingly the administrative infrastructure of seeking private donations became more evident at the school.

During the 1980s, and even more so in campaigns in the 1990s and the first decade of the 21st century, the school increasingly emphasized fundraising beyond Waterloo Region. The contributions of major Canadian banks and oil corporations and other large companies emphasized the fact that Laurier students and research activities extended the influence of the school to the provincial and even national arena.

Back in 1973 when Peters agreed to serve as Laurier's first president, he said he intended to serve just one five-year term. In 1978, as that term concluded, he could look back with pride on changes since the school made the transition from a Lutheran university to a public institution. Enrolment increased significantly, four buildings were erected, new graduate and undergraduate programs were introduced and Laurier became a successful part of the Ontario university community.

Dr. Neale Tayler, whose work as chair of romance languages, first chair of Graduate Studies and vice-president academic all spoke to his qualifications, emerged as the board's chosen successor to Frank Peters.

Archaeology's Norman Wagner was initially named to replace Tayler as academic vice-president, but in a short time he left to become the president of the University of Calgary. This time the opening was filled by economics Professor John Weir. When Peter Benton was selected as vice-president of finance, replacing Tamara Giesbrecht who had taken early retirement, a new team—a triumvirate that would run the university for the following four years—was in place.

In a 1998 interview with Librarian Eric Schultz, Weir said the three administrators agreed that Laurier's survival depended on their ability to expand enrolment across the university community as much as in the School of Business and Economics. "It was important to decide what the university was going to be," Weir explained. Being a small school in the same city as a big school meant that increasing enrolment and higher standards were important challenges. The combination of financial pressure and academic circumstance meant the university faced a choice: "We could cut costs or we could expand."

While examining their options, Weir visited a university in Oshkosh, Wisconsin, which had just finished a lengthy downsizing. After touring the campus he asked his hosts if they would choose the same option again. No, they said, the trauma associated with downsizing outweighed its financial benefits. Weir took the message to heart.

The decision not to downsize made expanded enrolment even more critical, but campus space was limited. For some time the university had considered constructing a professional building to house the School of Business and Economics, and near the end of Peters' term

ABOVE: Opening of the Frank C. Peters Building, 1980.

the province finally agreed to a funding proposal for a 73,000-square-foot building at University Avenue and Albert Street. After Peters' retirement, it was announced that the new building would bear his name, and in February 1980, it was officially opened by then Premier William Davis. In his remarks, the premier celebrated the success of the business school, but spoke of the fundamental value of a general education and expressed support for the Faculty of Arts as well.

A practical benefit of the new building was that for the first time in several years, Laurier functioned without portable classrooms. In September 1978, the university experimented with delivering education to students via a "tele-college" cable television program available in Kitchener, Waterloo, Cambridge, Stratford and Wilmot and Woolwich townships. The idea was to offer the opportunity for university courses to many people who would not have the chance to attend traditional classes.

Two courses selected as the initial tele-college offering, broadcast four nights a week at 7:30 p.m., were taught by two of Laurier's most talented and popular professors. Ralph Blackmore taught Economics 100 Monday and Wednesday evenings; Donald Morgenson taught Psychology 100 Tuesdays and Thursdays. All the lectures were repeated on Sundays and on the last Thursday of each month. Both professors took questions from viewers on a live phone-in program.

The courses were available as regular credits for all those who registered and paid the normal $150 course fee. But of course anyone could watch the lectures and they provided an exhilarating taste of university life for many viewers. Within two years, the tele-college program moved to TV Ontario and the schedule was expanded to 27 university credit courses, including not only business and psychology but also economics, political science and English.

The shift to TVO expanded the number of potential students and as Fred Little, Laurier's director of continuing education, said, the relationship with TVO "will make it possible for many thousands of people to begin the university courses in their home, and that's a real asset to many people, and almost everyone when winter weather makes long drives to campus difficult."

Little saw the program as a way for Laurier to give a second chance to people who had dropped out of school. "Such people have proved over and over again that they make excellent students," he said. Fees for students enrolling for credit were $81.50 for each one-term, half-credit course, or $163 for a two-term, full-credit course. With a goal of eventually allowing students to complete all the courses required for a degree through tele-college, combined with extension courses in summer school, a Laurier education became accessible to a broad range of Ontario students.

New buildings and new faculty were predicated on expanding enrolment. Each fall, the numbers were released and explained, greeted with pride at the steady rise amid some concern about the implications of an ever-bigger campus. In 1981, a five-year report on enrolment by Registrar James Wilgar said that of all Ontario universities, Laurier had experienced the most consistent annual increase in applications from graduating high school students. By 1981, its full-time enrolment was 4,006, compared to about 2,900 in 1976. Part-time numbers in the same period went to more than 3,100 from about 2,800. In total, after the five years, Laurier had 7,135 students.

....

When Ralph Blackmore arrived at Waterloo Lutheran University in 1966 to teach in the Economics Department, an arts faculty colleague told him, "I hope you didn't give up a good job to come here — this place has no future."

That colleague was wrong and Blackmore was one of the reasons. Blackmore was born in 1916 in Windsor, Ontario, and graduated from Ascension College in that city. As a young man, Blackmore combined education with a passion for boxing, becoming the Canadian Intermediate Middleweight Boxing champion of 1940. In 1945, while serving in the military, he won the Eastern Canadian Armed Services Middleweight Championship. After the war, Blackmore achieved a master's degree in economics from the University of Michigan and returned to Toronto to work at *The Globe and Mail*. He spent most of the next 10 years working in the business and finance sections, eventually attaining the position of financial editor.

After a brief sojourn owning a weekly paper in Streetsville, Ontario, and time in the public relations department of Massey Ferguson, Blackmore became assistant to the dean of York University's Atkinson College. In 1966, Herman Overgaard met Blackmore and invited him to join the faculty at Waterloo Lutheran. Blackmore quickly became one of the university's favourite professors, lecturing with passion and humour about economics, lectures he often illustrated with a copy of *The Globe and Mail*.

In addition to academic work, Blackmore became well-known to Kitchener and Waterloo residents for his regular appearances on CKCO-TV. Beginning in 1973, he hosted a late-evening interview segment called *Conversations* and for many years a Sunday-evening commentary called *Blackmore's Viewpoint*. In the late 1980s, Blackmore had a morning newscast on radio station CKKW.

Not only a gifted lecturer, Blackmore was an innovator as well, developing the now-famous Wilfrid Laurier University stock market game. He was also a pioneer in the university's tele-college program. Blackmore died in 2002, leaving behind several generations of students with fond memories of the professor.

RALPH BLACKMORE

President Tayler was gratified by Laurier's popularity, but concerned about it losing the close student-faculty relationships for which it was known, and worried about its limited facilities. In the fall of 1981, Laurier announced a plan to reduce its freshmen enrolment. As Wilgar said at the time, "we don't have the physical capacity to respond to the growth in applications nor could we admit more students without harming our faculty-student ratio and straining the dining hall, Library and other facilities." The required grade for admission to the School of Business and Economics reached 76 per cent; in other programs it was 62, up from the previous 60 per cent. Despite the registrar's determination, the following first-year class of 1,400 was the largest in the history of the institution. The total of 4,000 full-time undergraduates, 182 graduate students and 2,600 part-time students had the university bursting at the seams.

By 1986, when Laurier celebrated its 75th anniversary, undergraduate enrolment had grown to almost 4,500, supplemented by 350 graduate students and more than 2,500 part-time and extension students. Admission to the School of Business and Economics required a high school average of 79 per cent, while other faculties set a minimum average of 70.5 per cent.

Provincial funds allowed the university to expand dramatically in this period, but the budget was carefully considered and a surplus recorded in each year of the presidency of Neil Tayler and his successor in 1982, John Weir. In his interview with Schultz, Weir discussed the idea put forward by critics that salaries were deliberately kept low with a view to building a surplus. He said the difficulty of forecasting enrolment and the nature of some expenses meant the size of the surplus could not be predicted.

However, he also believed it was important to avoid a financial crisis. Reserves were necessary because he feared any financial crisis increased the risk that Laurier would be absorbed by the University of Waterloo. "I was never sanguine about the University of Waterloo," Weir said. The success of the 1970s and '80s meant there were fewer jokes at the University of Waterloo about "the high school down the street," but Weir continued to worry that a significant financial problem might encourage the provincial government to merge the two universities, with the resulting loss of Laurier's unique nature.

Weir was, in his own words, "not a hands-off president." During his term, he faced the usual challenges of maintaining the flow of funds and addressing enrolment questions, but he was also forced to confront new types of issues.

Weir served under several chancellors and noted they could play two different roles, one being to leverage successful fundraising, the other to increase the university's profile. The best do both. In this regard, John Black Aird, Weir's first chancellor, was very successful. Aird had contacts in the banking and energy sectors and used them to help launch Laurier's successful fundraising campaign in the early 1980s.

Noted soprano Maureen Forrester was an example of a high-profile chancellor. Her fame brought international attention to Laurier, but her hectic touring schedule meant that she was less available than Aird had been. However, when Forrester was on campus, Weir said, she was a fully involved and intense presence, especially in the Music Faculty.

Willard Estey's term as chancellor was less effective in fundraising, but Weir found his engagement in the day-to-day operation of the campus and his endless curiosity about improving the institution were valuable.

During Weir's presidential term, the university building campaign continued, funded in part by Aird's successful fundraising. In 1986, Aird's role not only as a fundraiser but also an adviser to the university was honoured with the naming of the new building which was to house the Music Faculty. The John Black Aird Arts Centre primarily provided space for recital and practice halls and an art gallery, but was expanded to include Faculty of Social Work offices. This reflected two important points, one being that Weir and the administration felt it was important to move Social Work out of the seminary building. The seminary was independent of the university and served a different function. Social work faculty members did not particularly like the decision, nor did music professors appreciate the incursion into their space, but Weir told both it was important that new buildings serve multiple purposes.

That said, Weir thought it was important to recognize the Faculty of Music and provide the space they needed. For him, the Faculty of Music represented the best values of the university. Although its enrolment was small, it meant a significant connection to the community and sent a message that Laurier cared about the arts.

Each new building had its own issues. In 1985, Laurier had opened a new women's residence. Much to Weir's regret, funding and time constraints meant the university opted for a traditional dormitory design rather than the newer style of residence apartments. Naming of the new residence, which had room for 140 women, reflected one of the great tragedies in the university's history. During an orientation event held at Bingeman Park in Kitchener in September 1985, student Brigitte Bouckaert suffered fatal injuries when she was hit by a bus transporting first-year students back to campus. In the traumatic aftermath, the university decided to name the new residence Bouckaert Hall. A coroner's inquest answered questions about the incident, but it did not lessen the community's devastation over her death.

In 1991, the new style of apartment residence was finally introduced to Laurier. Bricker residence was designed with four-bedroom suites, an innovation that proved tremendously popular with students and set a new standard for residence construction.

Bricker was a co-educational residence, which could be seen as the result of another incident in late September 1989, when a large group of male students launched a 4 a.m. panty raid on the women's residence. The following night, a group of female students responded with a raid on the men. It was by no means the first time raids had occurred on campus, but it would be the last. Following the raids, the situation turned ugly with a display in the dining hall of garments smeared with substances designed to resemble blood, feces and semen, and slogans designed to embarrass the owners. National media attention ensued.

The incident in its entirety was portrayed by critics within and beyond the Laurier community as an example of how women were oppressed on campus. The controversy deepened when it was revealed that the university's security and residence staff, following guidelines in a manual issued by administrators, helped students organize the panty raids. In the aftermath, some students and faculty complained bitterly about the message sent by the university's involvement, while a number of other students of both genders argued the incidents were harmless fun that did no lasting damage.

However, there would be no more panty raids at Laurier. President Weir announced that henceforth, the training of residence staff and orientation programs would include segments on gender relations and definitions of date rape, sexual assault and equity questions. The new Laurier Women's Centre grew out of the demand for education on the types of issues the incident raised. Another outcome was the establishment of co-educational residences.

A more positive reflection of the university in the national press was achieved with the success of the school's athletics teams. In 1978, the Golden Hawks football team, led by running back Jim Reid, won the Yates Cup. Reid went on to represent Canada in the Can-Am Bowl game, played against U.S. university players under Canadian rules in Tampa, Florida. Despite the valiant effort of Reid and the Canadians, the Americans emerged victorious by a score of 22 to 7.

Tuffy Knight's long career as Laurier's athletic director and head football coach concluded in 1984, when he moved on to an administrative role with the Toronto Argonauts.

Knight's assistant, Rich Newborough, who took over as athletic director and coach, was aggressive in expanding the commitment to women's athletics, which paid almost immediate dividends. The women's curling team won the provincial title in 1985, the first championship for female athletes at Laurier. The women's soccer team won four straight provincial titles from 1989 to 1993, including a national championship in 1992.

In 1991, Newborough's term as head coach was rewarded with the first national football championship in school history when the Golden Hawks won the Vanier Cup. For Weir, nearing the end of his presidency, the Vanier Cup was a highlight, "a moving moment and a coming-of-age."

In almost two decades following the attainment of provincial status, Wilfrid Laurier University went from being a small liberal arts college with a successful business school to a much larger, more dynamic educational institution. The student body increased, the faculty grew and the campus expanded as new buildings were completed on the 11-acre property at King Street and University Avenue. As it prepared to greet the 1990s, Laurier had survived a few embarrassing challenges and the many struggles of continuous growth. Despite John Weir's fears to the contrary, its place in the Ontario university community was secure, and under a new president, Lorna Marsden, a new era was about to begin.

ABOVE: Premier William Davis on campus, 1980.

ABOVE: President Lorna Marsden at convocation.

CHAPTER NINE
GROWTH AND CONSEQUENCES

A S THE 1990s BEGAN, Wilfrid Laurier University had enjoyed 17 years of enrolment growth and building expansion. The sought-after benefits of provincial funding had indeed paid dividends. However, Ontario's education world was beginning to change.

Laurier had maintained at least a small surplus each year, but that would be increasingly difficult with the new decade's economic realities. No longer a small school, it had almost 9,000 full- and part-time students putting stress on the physical plant and the faculty. To this mix was added a sense that spending, even in areas like education, needed to be restrained.

As the decade proceeded, Laurier continued to grow, but the implications of growth and pressures of funding created difficult situations for the administration, students, faculty and staff. The university was brought to public attention on numerous occasions, sometimes positively as with favourable rankings in *Maclean's* magazine later in the decade, but sometimes with issues requiring difficult choices and occasionally unpleasant decisions.

Perhaps nothing signified the new era more clearly than the process by which John Weir's successor as president was selected. For the first time since the arrival of William Villaume in 1961, the Board of Governors looked outside the Laurier community for a candidate.

Lorna Marsden's appointment as the first woman president began with the hiring of Janet Wright & Associates to conduct a search and identify a candidate. Marsden had met Wright on an airplane and they shared a taxicab from the airport to downtown Toronto. Over the course of their conversation, Marsden's suitability for the Laurier position became evident to Wright.

Marsden, a native of British Columbia, was a Liberal senator at the time. Prior to her Senate appointment, she had been a sociology professor and associate dean of the graduate school at the University of Toronto. Marsden remembered that John Black Aird, a former chancellor of Wilfrid Laurier University, had told her on her appointment to the Senate that her good work would be done within 10 years. At the time of meeting Wright, Marsden had served in the Senate more than seven years and she felt ready for a change.

Once appointed, Marsden decided a focus of her time in office would be the strengthening of academic programs. She recognized the importance of the Faculty of Music and was determined to increase the support provided to it. In addition, areas of the arts such as archaeology and anthropology called out for an increased commitment.

She was aware of the strong liberal arts and humanities tradition of Laurier, but she also believed the gradually increasing strength of the Science Department should be accelerated. Construction of a science building and the introduction and expansion of a grad program in science were important.

Marsden also acknowledged the influence and reputation of the School of Business and Economics, but believed in a balance in enrolment, which meant more emphasis on

ABOVE: John Weir, Bob Astley and Lorna Marsden at the announcement of her term as Laurier's first woman president.

recruitment for science and the arts. She thought the university should not grow too large. Increased enrolment should only be accompanied by an increase in the minimum grade level required for admission, a perspective that would require more vigorous fundraising by the university to replace the grants that additional new students would have generated.

Marsden was successful in urging the university's alumni not just to make personal donations, but to provide an entrée to corporate giving.

Fundraising was now a constant factor in the administration of the university. At the end of March 1995, a two-year effort called *Campaign Laurier* was launched, raising close to $16 million for the university. A celebration of its success in September 1997 was marked by a ceremony declaring Marsden an honorary alumna for her efforts.

The eclectic and impressive array of donors was exemplified by a Bell Canada donation of $350,000 and the Royal Bank of Canada's $250,000.

The largest donation, however, came from undergraduate students at Wilfrid Laurier University who, through their Student Union, pledged $3.1 million to be raised over 10 years. Their donation marked a continuing tradition: Laurier's Student Union has actively assisted in fundraising and consistently been a major contributor through special fees assessed to the student body for development purposes.

Even before Marsden took office, the provincial emphasis on restraint meant the university was facing a significant challenge in balancing revenue with spending. In 1992, a budget of $57.4 million resulted in a $3.2-million budget shortfall. News releases called it the most serious crisis to face the university since becoming a public institution 20 years earlier. Course offerings were cut back, the number of part-time stipends was reduced, and first-year and part-time admissions were trimmed.

The following year, the 1993 budget of $59.2 million forecast revenue of about $58.2 million, leaving a deficit in the area of $1 million. To cope, the administration eliminated four full-time equivalent faculty positions, extended part-time cuts to the equivalent of 4.3 full-time appointments and cancelled 12 full-time, non-faculty positions. As well, the university raised tuition by seven per cent.

By the time the April 1995 budget was established, Laurier had reduced its anticipated spending to $57.2 million. However, tuition increases of 10 per cent for new students and nine per cent for returning students would be necessary. In October 1995, a hiring and promotion freeze was put in place about the same time as the university announced it had closed out the previous year with a $7,000 surplus.

November 1995 marked two milestones, one positive, the other challenging. First, the November 12 issue of *Maclean's* magazine ranked Laurier fourth among primarily undergraduate universities. The celebration was short-lived: two weeks later, a "mini budget" from Ontario's new Conservative government instituted post-secondary education cutbacks that would cost Wilfrid Laurier University between $6 million and $8 million in grants, which was in addition to a $1.2-million reduction the province had announced earlier.

Also in the budget was an announcement that universities such as Laurier would be allowed to increase tuition by 10 per cent, with the power to levy a further 10-per-cent increase at their discretion.

In response, the university announced it would offer an early-retirement package for up to 60 staff and faculty members, and limit the renewal of contracts for non-permanent staff and faculty.

As a consequence, Laurier, along with many other provincial campuses, became the scene of regular protests against the government of Premier Mike Harris. While the impact on policy was limited, the rallies did focus the concerns of the entire post-secondary community.

In February 1996, Laurier announced that 40 staff and faculty had accepted the early-retirement offer. A month later, the administration announced a 15-per-cent increase in tuition for the following year.

The April 1997 university budget maintained the $57.4-million cost of operations and featured another 14.4-per-cent tuition increase. By the end of the decade, university finances were nearly balanced, and the 1999 budget called for revenue and expenditures of just under $66 million each.

In contrast to earlier years of enrolment cutbacks, the number of students began to rise again. In July 1998, a news release said "officials at Wilfrid Laurier are now dealing with a challenge any university might hope to face: how to accommodate a significant increase in the number of students who plan to attend in the fall." Despite higher tuition and budgetary pressure, Wilfrid Laurier remained a popular choice: full-time enrolment of 5,800 in 1990 had grown to well over 7,000 a decade later.

With budgets now ranging from $50 million to $60 million a year, Laurier struggled to maintain its labour relations traditions. From its earliest days, professors and staff had often been asked to make sacrifices in the interest of the institution. Negotiations, if there were any, tended to be on an individual basis, although general patterns in compensation and promotion developed.

Since the 1950s at least, there had been a Faculty Association at Waterloo College

ABOVE: President John Weir, Chancellor
Maureen Forrester and writer Edna Staebler.

and later Waterloo Lutheran University, but the association lacked the power to bargain collectively and acted more as a forum in which to express opinion than an entity that could be recognized as a labour union. By the late 1980s, it was clear this model was no longer sufficient for Laurier faculty. After much consideration, full-time faculty endorsed the decision to transform the Wilfrid Laurier University Faculty Association into a union to represent their interests through collective bargaining.

Staff members at Laurier were in a similar situation. The Staff Association created in the early 1970s was a social club rather than an agency for collective bargaining. As the organization grew, however, its relationship with the university developed and eventually included discussion of salaries and benefits, rudimentary grievance procedures and generally acting as a voice for staff within the Laurier community. By the mid-1990s it was seriously considering certification as a union. A special sub-committee was struck within the association to investigate the best way forward, which resulted in a decision to become an independent local union. On October 30, 1995, the Wilfrid Laurier University Staff Association became a trade union, and on May 14, 1997, the first collective agreement between the association and the administration was signed.

Looking back on this time, former President John Weir recalled his personal disappointment that faculty had felt the need to unionize, but he acknowledged that the formality and structure of the collective-bargaining process made many day-to-day operations of the university more transparent.

A number of other unions began to represent different sections of the wider Wilfrid Laurier community. The Canadian Union of Public Employees represent physical plant workers at the Waterloo and Kitchener campuses, the United Food and Commercial Workers Union speaks for food service workers and the International Alliance of Theatrical Stage Employees represents staff involved in music and theatrical productions.

Despite the financial obstacles imposed by budgetary restraint, Laurier enjoyed significant successes during Lorna Marsden's term and continuing through the rest of the 1990s. As early as 1992, the School of Business and Economics embarked on a new venture, offering a business diploma program in Trinidad and Tobago in co-operation with the Royal Bank of Trinidad and Tobago and the Institute of Business at the University of the West Indies. Local students could enrol for the business administration courses on a part-time basis.

Laurier had introduced a full-time Master of Business Administration program in 1986, but in 1994 it instituted a one-year MBA program that also proved to be very successful.

Also in 1994, a Science Building was opened, and the large, modern structure became a symbol of Laurier's stronger commitment to science under Marsden. Now science teaching and research could be carried out under one roof, and departments such as Biology, Physics and Psychology could expand their programs. As usual, numbers tell the story: in the 1993-94 school year, 267 undergraduates were enrolled in biology, but over the course of the decade that number would rise to more than 350. Other departments in the sciences saw similar growth.

In November 1998, the Senate met to consider a proposal to separate the Faculty of Arts and Science into two on the grounds that Arts and Science had grown too diverse to address the interests and concerns of individual constituents. The Senate approved, and in 2000 the Faculty of Science was launched with Dr. Art Szabo as its first dean.

One emerging development that seemed to contrast strongly with the early days of the university was the creation of co-operative programs with neighbouring institutions. Perhaps the most significant was the TriUniversity Group of Libraries. For years, Laurier had enjoyed a working relationship with libraries at the University of Guelph and the University of Waterloo, allowing users at each institution to borrow materials from any of the three and return them to the most convenient location.

As the 1990s progressed, cutbacks and fiscal restraint meant each library within the system had problems. Despite expansions, Laurier's Library was filled beyond capacity, while Guelph and Waterloo each filled most of their buildings plus rental space. The high cost of major serial collections meant many journals were being cancelled, although the libraries were under pressure to maintain their collections.

The province launched an incentive program to encourage inter-university co-operation in areas such as library holdings and the three university presidents agreed the concept was valid. In February 1995, President Marsden and two others signed an agreement to launch the TriUniversity Group of Libraries.

Another example of co-operation is found in the History Department. When Waterloo Lutheran University introduced Master of Arts programs in the 1960s, History explored the option. The department had grown, but not to the extent of offering a degree at the PhD level. That changed in 1994 when, after a series of talks with graduate departments at the University of Guelph and the University of Waterloo, the Tri-University Graduate Program in History came into existence. It allowed PhD students to benefit from the expertise of historians at all three universities while doing course work toward a degree.

The remarkably successful program inspired other arts departments to seek co-operative agreements. The Department of Geography and Environmental Science now offers a PhD program in collaboration with the University of Waterloo, as does the Department of Religion and Culture. The English Department offers a PhD program in co-operation with the University of Guelph. In each case, the universities and their students benefit from institutional co-operation to a degree that could not have been imagined in the 1960s.

While the academic offerings at Laurier expanded dramatically in this period, one area

ABOVE: Launch of the TriUniversity libraries group.

contracted and was eventually eliminated. The university's extension program, which had existed from the moment Waterloo Lutheran University became a separate institution, began to see dwindling attendance and interest by the early 1990s. The Ontario government program to encourage teachers to upgrade their qualifications had accomplished its goal and new teachers were no longer hired unless they had the appropriate university degree. President Marsden decided the program had outlived its usefulness: Laurier should focus on its core strengths and the extension program was no longer one of them.

As enrolment increased in the 1990s, students began to have a more significant impact on the neighbourhood around them. In some respects the influence was positive: more students leasing rooms and apartments meant their rent money flowed into the community. In other aspects, the influence was less positive.

In April 1994, a series of end-of-term house parties on Ezra Street, a short side street one block off campus, spilled outside and got out of hand, resulting in damage to property and complaints to police. The Student Union and university administrators encouraged students toward more responsible behaviour and worked with police and the community to attempt to ward off similar incidents.

But the following spring, *The Kitchener-Waterloo Record* reported that the city's biggest-ever street party would be held April 22 on Ezra Street. Student Union leader Ralph Spoltore was quoted as saying, "My personal feeling is that it's going to be a Junior Woodstock" and he predicted attendance would exceed 1,600 students. Police warned there would be zero tolerance of violations such as public drinking or littering. The party turned ugly and 42 people were arrested, including 18 Laurier students. Nine criminal charges were laid, as well as a plethora of liquor offences and noise violations. More seriously, a local woman was struck in the face by a piece of concrete thrown by one of the party-goers. In the end, more than 50 police officers swept down Ezra Street, restoring order and arresting anyone who refused to leave.

The community, university officials and the police all expressed anger and frustration over what had happened. The relationship between the City of Waterloo and the university was strained when a special council meeting watched videotape of police officers being assaulted and beer bottles smashed.

In the days that followed, the university decided on firm action. The 18 students arrested or charged by Waterloo Regional Police were sent letters, signed by President Marsden, informing them that they were required to appear before discipline hearings in mid-May. Marsden said that while the arrests and charges would be the responsibility of the appropriate civil authority, she had the right to initiate disciplinary proceedings.

Marsden was concerned that the future employment of Laurier graduates, placement of co-op students and the general perception of the Laurier community had been damaged. "The behaviour of those students involved has brought the university into disrepute and is prejudicial to the best interests of the university, its student body, its alumni and all those other citizens who are supporters of this institution," she said.

The disciplinary panel was made up of the president, the vice-president academic and other university leaders. Laurier's code of conduct allowed a range of penalties up to and including expulsion, withholding of grades or transcripts and prohibition against graduation at May convocation.

Eight students charged with offences under the Ontario Liquor Control Act were notified that their cases would be heard by a student disciplinary panel before any university disciplinary action was taken. That decision was somewhat controversial. Incoming Student Union President Scott McCormick acknowledged that the university calendar and student handbook both stated that student behaviour on and off campus could be acted on by the university, but McCormick thought the university's actions exceeded their legal authority. The university was unswayed.

Following the hearings, the university announced it would not reveal specific details about the sanctions or the number of students disciplined by the committee, but it was clear they had acted firmly in many cases. At least one student was denied the right to graduate. Several were placed on probation, and other disciplinary actions were put in place. "There are tasks they have to accomplish—we've tailored the punishment to fit the crime," President Marsden said.

The Laurier community approached the following April anxious that the events of 1994 and 1995 not be repeated. Laurier's plan was to hold an on-campus party designed to keep the celebration under control and within the boundaries of the university. Days prior to the party, Waterloo Regional Police arrested eight Laurier students, charging them with liquor violations and seizing kegs of beer and other alcohol from two houses near campus.

The on-campus party attracted 1,700 students and for the first time in several years Ezra Street was relatively quiet. By 1997, the campus party seemed like a tradition and the Ezra Street debacle faded into the past. The determined university response, both in terms of student discipline and the planning of an alternative event, and the help of the Student Union brought an end to the era of loud late-night street parties.

Laurier's success on sports fields and on ice garnered entirely positive reviews. During the 1990s, the Hawks met victory in a wide range of sports, in particular women's soccer where Laurier had a string of successes punctuated by national championships in 1992 and 1995. During the 1994-95 school year, Laurier introduced women's ice hockey to the roster of teams competing in the Ontario University Athletic Association roster, and within five years the women won their first ice hockey provincial championship, setting the stage for a remarkable run in the first decade of the new millennium.

President John Weir had described athletics as a bridge between the community and the university, and the successful Laurier teams and the enthusiasm with which they were greeted helped maintain the good relationship the university enjoyed with the City of Waterloo.

The other area which Weir considered a bridge was the music program. The opening of the Aird Centre and the expansion of facilities there for Laurier's music students improved their ability to reach out to the community. Perhaps the greatest evidence of this success is found in the relationship between the university and the Penderecki String Quartet. Founded in Poland in 1986, the group became Quartet in Residence at Laurier's music program in the mid-1990s.

The quartet performs a range of music from Bach to Frank Zappa and regularly plays works by new composers. One of the quartet's most valuable contributions to Laurier and the wider musical community is the International Intensive Chamber Music Course and Concert series, an event popularly known as QuartetFest. Hosted by the Penderecki Quartet, it brings renowned string artists from Canada, the United States and beyond to participate in master classes on the Laurier campus.

In 1997, Lorna Marsden announced she would not seek a second term as president, choosing instead to accept an appointment to the presidency of York University. Marsden left with good memories of Laurier, recalling that "while I was president, we acquired magnificent drawings and paintings by (Mennonite artist) Woldemar Neufeld and the support to house and look after them. It was a big undertaking for us in that financial climate, and we had so much encouragement and help from community members." Successes like that, plus the acquisition and renovation of a handsome heritage property known as Lucinda House across Albert Street from the campus provided Marsden's term with more than milestones. They were symbols of Laurier's integration into the history of its community.

ABOVE: Composer Barrie Cabena with music students.

ABOVE: President Max Blouw, Chancellor
John Pollock, and former President Robert
Rosehart.

CHAPTER TEN
TOWARD THE CENTENNIAL

R OBERT ROSEHART, MORE COMMONLY known within the Laurier community
as Builder Bob, succeeded Lorna Marsden as president in September 1997. Rosehart
had served 13 years as president and vice-chancellor of Lakehead University in Thunder
Bay, and was familiar with Waterloo Region after earning three degrees, including a PhD
in chemical engineering, at the University of Waterloo.

Rosehart's term spanned the transition from the late 1990s to the 21st century, a period
of rapid change that saw Laurier's expansion to a new campus in Brantford. At times,
the explosive growth threatened to exceed both the expectations and the capacity of
the university, and there were difficult questions to consider as Laurier approached its
centennial in 2011.

The university's academic *Century Plan* argued that Laurier's future was as a comprehensive university offering a wide range of undergraduate and graduate programs and professional schools. It was definitely a departure from the tradition of the small liberal arts college with a business program that had been the image of the school in the entire post-war period. The transition wasn't always smooth, and questions were raised about the wisdom of such policies and the capacity of the Laurier community to adapt to the new vision. Meanwhile, the pattern of growth that had been a steady factor in the university's history accelerated through this period, and eventually limited the options available to the school.

Much of the challenge that faced Laurier, and other Ontario universities in this period, derived from government funding policies that prompted schools to increase levels of enrolment in order to maintain services. The percentage of university operating costs covered by provincial grants has not kept pace with the increase in university expenses, and additional provincial funding has been tied to enrolment increases. This has created a situation in which enrolment increases, as well as increases in tuition fees and other fees charged to students, must make up the difference. While this places a strain on individual students to be able to afford university education, it also forces universities to rely on ever-increasing numbers of students to maintain balanced budgets. Laurier President Max Blouw, who succeeded Rosehart on September 1, 2007, has described this funding situation as a "growth treadmill," referring to the need for universities to take in more students in order to receive sufficient increases in provincial funding to pay for the increasing costs of running the university. This equation would influence a great deal of the university's thinking as the centennial year approached.

The driving force in Laurier's expansion was the unprecedented pace of full-time undergraduate enrolment. Increased enrolment was accompanied by a dramatic increase in teaching and residence facilities in both Waterloo and Brantford as the university desperately tried to keep up with its increased population. Faculty size also increased, although it failed to keep pace with the escalating enrolment.

One statistic provided comfort as the university examined its rapid growth. In May 1999, an Ontario study showed that 70.8 per cent of students who started in first-year

university in 1990 had graduated by 1997. Laurier's rate was 82 per cent, showing that although enrolment was increasing, the university experience was successful for most students.

In 1990, there were 5,800 full-time students at Laurier. By 1997, there were 7,000, with almost 1,300 more expected in 1998. Indeed, in the five years leading to the new millennium, full-time undergraduate enrolment increased by 52.4 per cent, outpacing even Ontario's expectation.

Under the province's "corridor system," Ontario set a minimum and maximum number of students each university was expected to enrol. As long as enrolment was within its established parameters, the university received 100 per cent of the government's per-student grant. If it exceeded the maximum, the province would not provide grants for the additional students.

By 2001, 15 per cent of Laurier's undergraduate numbers were above its corridor maximum, meaning tuition fees were the only money the university would receive for them. Laurier estimated the lost grants to be worth $6 million to $7 million.

As new students arrived at the university the number of full-time faculty also increased. The rate of increase for faculty significantly trailed the increase in student body, however.

Full-time faculty in the period between 1996 and 2001 increased by about 23.9 per cent, going from 264 to 327 faculty members. Part-time faculty members, expressed in full-time equivalents, increased from 39 to 48 or about 23 per cent. Graduate full-time enrolment had increased over the same period by about 9.3 per cent, reflecting the smaller graduate faculties. That was to change as well, however, as in the new millennium Laurier expanded the graduate programs significantly.

Dramatic growth came at a cost. When the autumn 2001 term began, crowding was almost unbearable. Hallways and staircases were packed. The dining hall struggled to cope and residences were so over-booked that the university offered students a BlackBerry smartphone or computer if they withdrew from residence.

At a public meeting called by the Student Union to discuss the situation, students complained about three students being squeezed into a residence room designed for two, 15-minute waits in the dining hall line and classrooms without enough seats. First-year enrolment had exceeded expectations by more than 320 people, and the university was scrambling to adjust, but some conditions the students described surprised even the administration. The student-faculty ratio, which had been 23 to one in 2000, jumped in a year to 23.7 to one.

The students' town hall meeting really just confirmed the obvious. *Maclean's* magazine data at the time of the meeting showed that of 47 Canadian universities, Laurier was the 27th largest. "We are not a small school anymore, we are a mid-size school," Vice-President Academic Roland Smith said, adding it had been true for some time. Smith said he sympathized with people who "see their own idea of their institution evaporating."

The student town hall called for an enrolment freeze, arguing the university had exceeded its capacity. In the circumstances of the early 2000s, however, a freeze was unlikely. As Rosehart explained, some pressure would be relieved by the aggressive building campaign the university had undertaken, but he warned students and the university community that a great new influx of students was on the horizon because of what was known as the "double cohort."

The double cohort was due to Ontario's decision to abandon Grade 13, meaning there would be one year, 2003, in which the first of the Grade 12 stream and the last of the

Grade 13 stream would overlap and graduate at the same time, potentially doubling the number of university applicants for that fall.

In 2002, Laurier anticipated taking in about 2,200 first-year students, the same as in 2001, but in 2003, with the double cohort, first-year admissions would top 2,700. "That's not negotiable," Rosehart said, explaining that, as a public university, Laurier had a moral responsibility to take in more students.

However, part of Laurier's dramatic growth was based on the new campus in Brantford, Ontario, a project sparked by a visit there by history Professor Terry Copp in the mid-1990s. In Brantford's deteriorating downtown, Copp saw potential for the community to provide a home for a new satellite campus for Laurier. It would offer relief from the constraints of limited space in Waterloo as well as hope for a community in decline.

Copp contacted a former student, Rob Campbell, now a principal with the Brantford separate school system, and arranged to meet with the mayor of Brantford. The positive mood of the meeting attracted President Rosehart's attention and his support for the satellite campus idea.

Leo Groarke's book, *Reinventing Brantford: A University Comes Downtown,* offers a detailed discussion of the development and expansion of the Brantford project, recounting the excitement and also the many problems that faced the university community and the City of Brantford as they examined the possibility of a new campus.

After much discussion within the Laurier administration about the viability, or even desirability, of a new campus, the school took on the challenge and moved forward, aiming to open it in 1999. Arthur Read, the long-time dean of arts and sciences, was chosen to be the first dean at Brantford.

Read was attracted to the community's vacant ICOMM centre, a large modern building that had been constructed as a telecommunications facility. Laurier's ambitions for the building, however, were undermined by a decision to open a casino there. The alternative to the ICOMM centre was Brantford's Carnegie Library. The old building would require a great deal of renovation before it was suitable, but it did provide a visually compelling image of the institution that Laurier Brantford could become.

Negotiations with the city were not easy. Gradually a consensus emerged that a

ABOVE: Ribbon-cutting ceremony for the Laurier Brantford campus, September 1999.

Brantford campus was a good idea, but one challenge was the Ontario government's reluctance to invest in the capital construction of a campus. Despite presentations by both the city and Laurier, the province refused any funding other than the per-student subsidy. Proceeding without the province would place a considerable burden on the taxpayers of Brantford and create doubt about whether Laurier Brantford could succeed.

In the fall of 1999, Arthur Read and a small group of dedicated staff and faculty launched the new campus in the Carnegie building. Overcoming the challenge of underfunding was one thing, but the potentially disastrous difficulty of attracting students to a new, seemingly undefined university experience resulted in the greatest victory of the first year. Read's easy manner and friendly persuasion helped sell Laurier Brantford to high school students and the community, a process bolstered by a university decision to offer scholarships to new students.

Laurier also decided to offer students applying unsuccessfully to the Waterloo campus the opportunity to enrol at Brantford if their marks were just short of the Waterloo admission standard. Finally, major recruiting efforts were launched in the Brantford area and beyond as the risk that low enrolment presented to the future of the new campus became apparent.

In planning curriculum for the Brantford campus, Vice-President Academic Roland Smith and Dean Read agreed on the importance and value of liberal arts as the foundation. The circumstances at Brantford, with a small campus and limited facilities, seemed to suit that focus, but there was some discussion about the appropriateness or viability of a traditional education in the new setting. The solution, after much discussion, proved to be a new study program called "contemporary studies."

The mission statement for Brantford stated that the campus was dedicated to the liberal arts and sciences which would provide students with skills and knowledge relevant to contemporary issues. The contemporary studies curriculum drew from a wide range of traditional disciplines, presenting them in a new interdisciplinary way. It also had the benefit of creating a series of courses that did not directly compete with more traditional offerings at the Waterloo campus. Such non-competition might prove untenable in the long run, but initially it was seen as a selling point for the Brantford campus.

With the disappointing initial enrolment numbers at Brantford, however, some within the Waterloo campus began to consider if alternative approaches were needed. One key solution turned out to be a different method of educating future teachers. Rosehart looked to an innovative co-operative venture, entering into an agreement with Nipissing University to provide the new form of teacher education. Extensive negotiations between Rosehart and Nipissing President David Marshall resulted in the creation of Ontario's first concurrent education program, combining a contemporary studies degree with a Nipissing degree in education. Students spent part of each term in a teaching practicum with local schools and graduated with considerably more classroom experience than might otherwise have been the case.

The program was launched in September 2002, and proved to be extremely successful. The attraction of the education program and the gradual success of other courses at Brantford triggered enrolment increases of 70 to 100 per cent per year and the recruitment crisis faded.

At both the Brantford and Waterloo campuses, the rapid influx of new students meant new residence and teaching facilities. In 2005, the university's *Century Plan* looked over a decade of building on both campuses with pride. Construction included a Library

SPIRIT OF THE PURPLE AND GOLD

In assessing the degree of success or failure of modern post-secondary education, one phrase that has come to be used frequently is "student engagement."

Engagement is generally measured by students' satisfaction with their educational experience. By these criteria, the Wilfrid Laurier University record is strongly positive. In 2006, following a continent-wide survey of undergraduate students at first-year and senior levels, the National Survey of Student Engagement concluded that Laurier scored above the provincial average in almost every key area.

Perhaps the most important result for Laurier was the question of whether students starting over would attend the same institution. More than half of Laurier's first-year students and 46 per cent of the seniors said definitely yes. In both cases, the response was more than 10 per cent higher than the provincial average.

At Laurier, however, student engagement always meant something more than what might be called customer satisfaction. Remembering her years at Laurier, former president Lorna Marsden remarked that from the start of orientation week, the university and the student body worked together to infuse newcomers with what she called the Spirit of the Purple and Gold. Clearly they were successful.

The orientation week tradition of Shinerama, a national fundraiser to support cystic fibrosis research

that was launched by a Waterloo Lutheran student 50 years ago, communicates that the purpose of the week is not just to welcome Laurier students to their new school, but to introduce them to the concept of the university as a vehicle for community improvement. Similarly, almost from its inception, Winter Carnival has been used not simply to entertain students, but also to raise money and awareness.

According to the North American student survey, by the time they are seniors, more than 62 per cent of Laurier students say they have done community service or volunteer work, a number that compares favourably with other institutions in Canada and reflects something of the spirit Marsden described.

In 2004, Laurier decided to provide some official recognition of co-curricular work, and students were able to register their efforts in a manner that validated their contribution through an official Co-curricular Record. Since that point more than 4,000 students have taken advantage of the opportunity and the co-curricular program continues to expand.

Laurier has always relied on its students. In fundraising efforts, the Student Union is traditionally a leading contributor, often the largest. Student mentors and volunteers help make the school a success, and student engagement has always had meaning beyond what a survey can calculate.

renovation, expansion and renovation of the Athletic Complex and an extensive overhaul of the dining hall to improve both access and food selection. Health and Counselling Services were expanded and new residences, including the King Street and Waterloo College Hall residences, helped Laurier maintain its commitment to all first-year students that they could live in residence the first year if they wished.

New academic buildings were also opened. The Bricker Academic building, a new teaching structure on Bricker Avenue, significantly increased the capacity of Laurier's teaching rooms. It was connected to the existing Science building by the new Science Research Centre, a dramatic new structure accommodating 95 researchers and more than 2,000 students of biology, chemistry, kinesiology, physical education, mathematics, psychology, physics and computer science.

The School of Business and Economics benefited from a $2-million donation by Robert and Myrna Schlegel for the construction of a centre for the study of entrepreneurship and technology. Robert Schlegel had graduated from Waterloo Lutheran University in 1972 with a degree in economics, and he and his wife enjoyed enormous business success in the United States. Robert, a chartered accountant, opened a business called Pavestone Co., while Myrna developed PeopleCare Heritage Centers. The Schlegels said they hoped their donation and the creation of the Schlegel Centre for Entrepreneurship would help students succeed through their personal "Triple E" formula for success: education, entrepreneurship and emotion.

The Schlegels' donation was important in financing the building campaign, but more donations were needed, and by far the greatest single contribution came from the province's SuperBuild fund. SuperBuild was responsible for some financing of the Schlegel building, upgrades to the Arts building and more than $11 million toward updates and construction of the Bricker Academic building and the Athletic Complex. The Science Research Centre and other buildings also benefited.

The major infusion of cash from the province was intended in part to help the university cope with the double cohort, but also to establish a sound infrastructure for the post-secondary education system. Funds also came from the federal government to help pay for the Science Research Centre. In each case, however, Laurier was required to contribute money, too, and in doing so accrued significant debt.

As Groarke's book indicates, SuperBuild funding for Laurier Brantford was a disappointment. The provincial program required the university to prioritize its funding applications and the ministry would not allow the Brantford and Waterloo campuses to submit separate proposals. Given the relative sizes of the two schools, Rosehart decided Waterloo projects must rank above the Brantford building campaign. As a result, SuperBuild bypassed Brantford.

From its beginning in the old Carnegie Library, the founders of the Brantford campus had looked out over Victoria Square and envisioned the campus spreading among the buildings of downtown Brantford. This vision, which would prove accurate as years passed, included Laurier purchasing or otherwise acquiring downtown buildings to house its new community. Without the benefit of provincial funding, this acquisition would require a significant community contribution and also the assumption of more debt by the university.

As enrolment grew, Laurier increasingly felt the stress of the province's reluctance to invest in capital costs of the satellite campus, although Brantford's building growth was at least as impressive as that of the Waterloo campus. From the start of the Brantford experience, Dean Arthur Read was aware that the school would quickly outgrow the Carnegie building, and the expansion he predicted happened almost immediately as the university moved into the old Odeon Theatre. In rapid succession, the university also expanded to the Post House residence, Grand River Hall residence and an expanded administrative and teaching facility within Grand River Hall.

As Groarke points out, a key part of the expansion of the Brantford campus was Laurier's new relationship with Mohawk College, which at the time was the other higher-education facility in Brantford. Under a unique agreement between Mohawk and Laurier, students attending either institution were able to take courses and apply their credits to a new sort of degree that allowed students to combine contemporary studies with Mohawk courses. The new program, called "Two By Four," allowed students to earn both a degree in contemporary studies and a college diploma in four years.

Among the benefits of the Two By Four program was that it reflected the spirit of

ABOVE: Students in front of the Schlegel Centre on the Waterloo campus.

co-operation between colleges and universities that the provincial government wanted to see. It also allowed Laurier to ease some of its spending concerns, and despite some reservations about the academic qualifications of college students entering the university segment of the program, for the most part the students and the program were a success.

The Mohawk collaboration and the agreement with Nipissing were prime examples of innovative new approaches to education at Brantford. To be sure, some of it was brought about by necessity as the Brantford campus struggled with achieving enrolment numbers that would be economically feasible in the long term, but they also reflected the desire of the Brantford community to do something distinctive, a goal which marked the campus from its beginning.

Laurier Brantford's decision to admit home-schooled students was similar. Home-schooling was illegal in Ontario prior to 2001, which is not to say it didn't happen, but in that year the provincial government recognized home-schooling as legitimate. To accommodate home-schooled students, Brantford took the innovative step of creating an admissions test to ensure that such students had achieved a level of education suitable for admission to university.

There were still more consequences of Laurier's dramatic growth. As the university became larger and more complex, so, too, did the campus labour situation. The new reality would lead to the first strike in the university's history.

In September 2002, in the midst of negotiations for a new contract, the Wilfrid Laurier University Staff Association voted more than 80 per cent in favour of strike action. The outstanding issue in the dispute was the ability of the university to contract out work traditionally done by union members. The issue would prove difficult to resolve. The staff association represented secretaries, telephone operators, student awards employees, the Registrar's office, Counselling and a wide range of other services. As *The Record* pointed out, the union represented "virtually every face a student sees outside the classroom."

The strike lasted eight weeks and the atmosphere on campus became strained as both sides appealed for the sympathy of the university community. This friction was reflected in an administration decision to hire an outside security firm and, at one point in the dispute, to videotape the pickets. The university eventually backed away from the plan,

ABOVE: Students on the Brantford campus.

but it reflected the sense of siege on both sides. During that period, mediation efforts by the province, as well as Luke Fusco, the dean of social work, failed to bring the two parties together. From September until November, pickets walked a line in front of the university buildings. Campus life was disrupted as never before.

Toward the end of the strike, Fusco, as mediator, suggested each side submit their disagreement to binding arbitration. While there was some agreement it might be the best course of action, they couldn't find middle ground on the terms for such a submission. In the end, Bruce Wolf, president of the staff association, and Jim Butler, vice-president of finance and Laurier's negotiator, decided to abandon arbitration and hash out an agreement themselves. After an all-night bargaining session, the two sides announced a settlement and in early November the university began, very slowly, to return to normal.

In the aftermath of the strike, hard feelings persisted. At a Board of Governors meeting, both faculty and staff representatives questioned whether the board had been sufficiently active in the dispute. The board consensus, however, was that their proper role was to

allow the administration to conduct its business.

Within the student body, there was criticism of both sides and disappointment that so much disruption had been tolerated. The university made some efforts to address the impact of the strike on students, but scars lingered for some time in almost every area. In the end, one side-effect was that Laurier experienced a net saving of $1.2 million in wages, which reduced the anticipated deficit for that year to $25,000. The news was small comfort, however, especially as Butler noted that while the strike had been settled, there were difficult financial times ahead.

Some of the lessons learned in the strike would come into play in 2008, six years later, when Laurier's Contract Academic Staff, often referred to as part-time instructors, went on strike. Significant numbers of contract employees was one result of the rapid expansion of student enrolment and limits on full-time faculty. By 2008, estimates were that more than 40 per cent of students were being taught by members of the Contract Academic Staff bargaining unit.

The unit had been officially recognized and achieved its first contract in 2000. The issues of the 2008 strike revolved around questions of seniority, job security and pay. Over the course of the two-week walkout, both sides placed their issues before the university community, and while the subsequent agreement addressed some problems, it did not change the university's dependence on contract academics. [2]

In the midst of growth and change and even turmoil, the reliable success of Laurier's athletic teams continued, and several particularly memorable teams merit special recognition. The women's hockey program at Laurier has enjoyed almost unparalleled success in recent years. Head coach Rick Osborne arrived in 2003 and promptly won a national championship. Between 1998 and early 2011, the women's hockey team won 10 Ontario championships and continues to do well at the national finals.

The women's lacrosse team has won eight provincial titles since 2000, including six in a row mid-decade. In the absence of a national championship for lacrosse, the women's team has achieved the ultimate success on a regular basis.

On the men's side, the highlight of the decade was clearly the 2005 Vanier Cup championship for the football team. The Golden Hawks had enjoyed an undefeated season in the march to the Vanier Cup and met another undefeated team, this one from Saskatchewan. In a dramatic game that saw the lead change sides five times, the Golden Hawks eliminated an eight-point deficit in the fourth quarter to take control with just 19 seconds left in the game.

Both the men's and women's curling teams thrived during this period, including three national championships for the women since 2007, and a national championship for the men in 2007-08.

University athletic programs have the advantage of bridging the university and the community with a fan base that extends beyond students on campus, and also creates a spirit of solidarity within the university. It's difficult for even the least focused of fans to avoid an emotional tug while watching the Golden Hawks succeed in competition, no matter what the sport. Laurier's community has been well served by its athletes and their success reflects well on the institution and its supporters.

At its core, the idea of a comprehensive university revolves around academic offerings, and those of Laurier underwent dramatic expansion undeterred by any sense of turmoil during enrolment growth or labour strife.

In its *Century Plan*, Laurier defined a comprehensive university as one with 30 graduate

[2] The author was one of the contract academics on strike in 2008.

programs, including 10 at the PhD level. By 2005, Laurier offered 11 master's-level and eight PhD programs. The university was well on track to achieve comprehensive status by 2011.

Aside from the goal of creating more graduate programs, Laurier's course offerings at undergraduate and graduate levels increased significantly in the decade leading up to the centennial. Brantford's contemporary studies program, the creation of a separate Faculty of Science and the elevation of kinesiology to degree status all contributed to the groundwork for an expanded university.

One significant element of Laurier's new millennium was the acquisition of the former St. Jerome's High School in downtown Kitchener. A partnership with the City of Kitchener allowed the renovation of the building as a new home for the Faculty of Social Work that had outgrown its location on the Waterloo campus.

For the first time since its inception, Social Work had a stand-alone facility that reflected its ambition and curriculum. The benefits of the new location accentuated the importance of a $1.5-million donation by the Lyle S. Hallman Foundation to create the Lyle S. Hallman chair in Child and Family Welfare. Gary Cameron was the initial recipient of the chair.

In 2000, the federal government introduced a program of Canada research chairs designed to increase the research capacity of Canadian universities. It is a measure of Laurier's increasingly academic focus that within several years five Laurier researchers held chairs, all but one of them in the sciences.

Laurier's traditional strength in the arts was reflected in Rhoda E. Howard-Hassmann's chair in International Human Rights, centred in the Global Studies and Political Science departments. Other chairs were in disciplines lodged in the Science building and the new Science Research Centre.

In August 2004, Roderick Melnick received a Tier 1 Canada research chair in Mathematical Modelling. He had been recruited from Denmark and arrived at Laurier to set up a program "analysing, modelling and simulating coupled systems, processes and phenomena, with applications in science and leading-edge technologies." Melnick's work involved significant international co-operation as well as involvement with various local institutions, including the Guelph-Waterloo Institute of Physics.

ABOVE: The Lyle S. Hallman Faculty of Social Work, in the former St. Jerome's High School in downtown Kitchener.

In psychology, Philip R. Servos received a Canada Research Chair in Cognitive Neuroscience. As a result, Laurier now hosts the Laurier Centre for Cognitive Neuroscience, observing the brain through magnetic resonance imaging to determine how it organizes information from different parts of the body. The centre brings together six researchers examining from different perspectives how the brain reacts in a variety of circumstances.

The Psychology Department is also home to a Canada Research Chair in Social Psychology, held by Anne Wilson who examines motivation and choice-making and attempts to understand why people make the choices they do.

Psychology also has a role in the Canada Research Chair in Group Dynamics and Physical Activity. Chair holder Mark A. Eys' research involves understanding how group membership in physical activity influences individual cognition and behaviour, and determining what makes sport and exercise groups effective. The chair incorporates kinesiology and physical education as well as psychology.

William Quinton in the Geography and Environmental Studies Department was another Canada Research Chair, this time in cold regions hydrology. Quinton's work uses

ABOVE: Mathematics professor Marc
Kilgour in class.

field, laboratory and modelling research to increase our ability to predict the cycling and storage of freshwater in headwater basins of the boreal and adjacent cold regions. The Research Chair added to success the Geography and Environmental Studies Department already enjoyed with its Cold Regions Research Centre, established in 1988. The centre consults on topics as varied as hydrology, climatology, glaciology, resource management, parks planning and biogeochemistry, and Quinton's work complements this achievement.

The significance of the Canada Research Chairs was not simply the attention they drew to Laurier and the contribution they made to research in Canada. The chairs also validated the role of Wilfrid Laurier as a research centre in the Canadian university community. The fact that much of the research was focused in the sciences showed Laurier's chosen direction was beginning to pay dividends.

Nor are Laurier's contributions to knowledge limited to federally funded chairs, as the Cold Regions Research Centre proves. Melnick's chair in mathematics is not that department's only research initiative. It is also home to Marc Kilgour, whose work with the Laurier Centre for Military, Strategic and Disarmament Studies used mathematics and gaming to help understand disarmament negotiations.

The military centre was founded in 1991 by Kilgour and Professor Terry Copp, one of Canada's leading military historians, with an initial grant of $70,000 a year for three years from the Department of National Defence. The grants, which were regularly renewed, allowed the centre to become a focus for the study of Canadian military history and the examination of conflict and conflict resolution around the world. The centre also publishes a journal, *Canadian Military History,* and conducts conferences and battlefield tours in Europe.

In the Political Science Department, the Laurier Institute for the Study of Public Opinion and Policy promotes research on public opinion in the political process. It also monitors public opinion and interest group industries, a process assisted by a donation of data from Ipsos Reid, a global market research firm. LISPOP, as the research institute is known, has particularly become known for Canadian election projections at the federal and provincial levels.

The Schlegel Centre for Entrepreneurship in the School of Business and Economics is just one of the many ways in which the school conducts in-depth research. The school is home to research centres for the study of accounting, supply chain management and financial services. For the most part these centres, like the military centre and the political research institute, serve not just an academic function but also provide services and information to the public. Their importance lies not just in the academic information they provide, but also in the recognition of Laurier as a source of research and development spanning the academic and popular communities.

The Faculty of Music introduced a new program, a Master of Music Therapy, in 2003. The department calendar describes it this way: "Music-centred, humanistic and integrated: theoretical aspects are incorporated into the development of clinical

techniques, both musical and humanistic." In practice, the program teaches students how to use music in various therapeutic settings and three on-site clinics provide master's students with practical experience. Recently the Faculty of Music announced the opening of a new facility, the Manfred and Penny Conrad Institute for Music Therapy Research, in recognition of the Conrads' gift of $1 million. The new institute will continue work in areas such as the connections between music, the brain and possible solutions to problems related to Parkinson's and Alzheimer's diseases.

All of the programs and the expansion mentioned above came with costs that could not be met by grants alone. The success of *Campaign Laurier* had not ended the need for fundraising and in the decade between 1997 and 2007 a renewed and aggressive campaign was launched, culminating in a celebration in November 2007 noting the raising of more than $100 million.

Corporate donations continued to be important, but as with previous campaigns the largest donations came from the Student Union. In addition, staff and faculty also made major donations. In announcing the impressive total, Vice-President of University Advancement Scott Hayter said the entire Laurier community, staff, faculty, students and even alumni would benefit from the infusion of capital. New academic programs, expanded fellowships, new buildings and improvements to existing facilities were all made possible by the campaign.

Furthermore, Hayter said, "more challenges lie ahead and the need for support is ongoing." In March 2011, the Student Union announced a new donation of $12.7 million to be spread over 10 years. Student Union President and CEO Kyle Walker noted that "this is the largest gift given to date to Laurier during its centennial, and we are pleased that it is from the students for the betterment of the students."

From the beginning of the college in 1911 through the expansion of the 1920s into the 1930s and the Second World War, the vital support of the Lutheran Synod tended to be sporadic and locally based. When major campaigns were launched, they were usually in reaction to an immediate and intense crisis.

In the modern era, fundraising is an ongoing process that has moved well beyond the boundaries of Waterloo Region. One factor remains consistent: those who contribute recognize that their community, be it local, national or even international, benefits from the success of the institution.

The *Century Plan's* definition of a comprehensive university requires the presence of a professional school. In 2006, Laurier was granted the right to operate a Faculty of Education. Making the announcement, Kitchener Centre MPP John Milloy, who was then parliamentary assistant to the provincial education minister, said, "For too long, a community of our size, which is also home to some 50,000 undergraduate students, has gone without direct access to a Faculty of Education. This important step towards a new teachers' college recognizes the quality of Waterloo Region's post-secondary institutions and the strength of our community."

The faculty, which opened in the fall of 2007, provides instruction for up to 90 elementary school teachers. Initially the province agreed to fund the program at a rate of about $10,000 per student, but provided no money for a new building. Laurier struggled to find a home and eventually placed the program in the Bricker Academic building. While some questioned the need for a new source of teachers in Ontario, the Laurier program developed in a unique way, building on close co-operation with four local school boards to place teaching students in classrooms at least once a week, as well as longer periods of practice teaching

As it approached its centennial Wilfrid Laurier University had expanded to encompass an enormous range of curricula. Brantford's programs in criminology and in journalism supplemented the existing contemporary studies program and expanded the offerings of the institution. At the Waterloo campus every faculty grew, both in undergraduate and graduate programs, as the university offered ever-wider ranges of opportunity to incoming students.

Bob Rosehart's successor, Max Blouw, has seen the university continue to expand during his term as president. Enrolment statistics for the year 2009 indicate that amongst all campuses and including full- and part-time students, enrolment at Wilfrid Laurier reached 16,588 students. That number continues to grow. Faculty numbers have increased dramatically as well. The 327 full-time faculty in 2001 became 460 by 2005, and in 2010 the number of full-time faculty was 516. Even more dramatic was the increase in part-time faculty which, expressed as full-time equivalents, went from 48 in 2001 to more than 177 in 2010.

The growth of Laurier can be measured not just in student enrolment or even in the growth of faculty, but also must be considered in the physical presence. Wilfrid Laurier University now encompasses the original campus in Waterloo, a second major campus in Brantford, a Kitchener building that houses the Faculty of Social Work, teaching facilities in Toronto that serve the School of Business and Economics' weekend MBA program, and a Toronto office that assists a wide variety of departments, from co-op services to development and alumni relations.

Meanwhile, new frontiers are opening. In 2007, Laurier opened an office in Chongqing, a district of more than 30 million people in southwest China, an area expected to grow significantly. Laurier personnel based at Chongqing University pursue opportunities for exchanges and collaboration with a range of academic institutions in the area.

Closer to home, Laurier recently entered into a memo of understanding with the Town of Milton, Ontario, a rapidly growing community on the edge of the Greater Toronto Area. Laurier hopes to open a satellite campus similar to Brantford in Milton, and President Blouw speaks of a future when Laurier will encompass three campuses, each with approximately 15,000 students. They would share a standard approach and be digitally connected, yet each campus would retain the feeling of a small- to medium-size

ABOVE: Grand opening of the Toronto office, September 2009.

university rather than the sprawling model of other comprehensive schools.

One of the side-effects of the rapid growth of the university is that questions which in earlier times might have been taken for granted now require wider and more careful examination before they are resolved. Two recent examples reflect the way in which the broader university community is now involved with more strategic questions about the institution's future.

The first example can be found in an ambitious task force introduced by President Blouw and charged with investigating multi-campus governance. In the early 1920s, governance was a simple matter. Weekly meetings of the entire faculty in the dean's office, occasional meetings of the Board of Governors, and an annual report to Synod covered every eventuality. Things have grown far more complex. President Blouw's task force explored many governance models by looking at campuses across Canada for inspiration and considering the unique circumstances at Laurier.

The result of this process was a series of 14 points of consensus that set out to establish the basic principles of a multi-campus future. Each point was relevant and important to the future development of the school, but the first two are perhaps most important. They confirm that the powers of the president, the Board of Governors and the Senate, as originally outlined in the legislation of 1973, remain in force. The second point enunciates the most important recommendation of the committee: "Laurier is one institution operating in multiple locations. The Wilfrid Laurier University degree is not distinguishable by location."

The task force report examined a number of challenges facing the university. Among these, one of the most important is the balance between the desires of the constituent parts for greater autonomy and the necessity for the institution to maintain a level of centralized control. As the university continues to evolve, and as its constituent campuses expand, these questions become more important.

The second exercise, which drew upon new methods to contemplate and plan for the university's future, was a process known as "Envisioning Laurier." When it opened its doors in 1911, the school that would become Wilfrid Laurier University did not require a mission statement. Its purpose was well-defined and understood: to educate young Canadian men as Lutheran ministers, thereby providing the Lutheran Church with a Canadian-based clergy. As time went on that purpose evolved, encompassing the introduction of arts courses, the provision of degrees and eventually the expansion into a full university.

The university had developed a mission statement and a statement of values in 1994, and it also produced a number of five-year university plans in the 1990s and into the 2000s. But shortly after becoming president in September 2007, Blouw said Laurier needed a more thorough understanding of itself and a clear vision for how it should develop and evolve over the next 30 years. "An organization as large and complex as a university can

RIGHT: "Sir Wilfrid" visiting the university that bears his name in the fall of 2008 as part of the Envisioning Laurier process to ask students, staff and faculty about their visions for the future.

LEADERSHIP AND PURPOSE

lumber along on momentum for quite some time," he wrote. "But to remain vibrant, to
ensure that growth is strategic and constructive, any organization requires a clear vision
of what it is and what it wishes to become."

Blouw felt it was important that the university community as a whole take time to
examine its purpose and its future. In the fall of 2007, he initiated the Envisioning Laurier
process which would, over the course of 12 months, develop and articulate a vision
statement for the school and a set of shared values and guiding principles to help govern
choices the school would make in the future. A key motivation for the visioning process
was clearly the rapid expansion the school had experienced in the previous decade. How
could the university continue to reflect the values upon which it had grown—values of
student engagement and community involvement—as it continued to increase in size?
Many on campus feared those traditional values would be diluted or lost in the multi-
campus university of the future.

As part of the consultation process, a national market research firm, The Strategic
Counsel, carried out a comprehensive research project with internal and external
audiences to assist the Senate committee in charge of the Envisioning Laurier initiative.
One goal was to establish benchmarking data that could be used in future to measure

what people locally and across the country know and think about the university. Virtually every component of the Laurier community participated in the process; opinions and discussions were cultivated in workshops and online forums, surveys and even less formal venues. By the fall of 2008, the committee was ready to report its results to the Senate, the Board of Governors and by extension the wider Laurier community.

The consensus, as committee member Dr. Mary-Louise Byrne noted, was that "there was a common passion around our distinct sense of community and the university's commitment to excellence in teaching, scholarship and research." Her colleague, Dr. Theresa Libby, said the consultation process had emphasized "the importance we all place on Laurier's sense of community and our willingness to be involved in ensuring the long-term success of our university."

On a practical level, one result was the articulation of fundamental values the participants hoped would underpin the university's development over the following 30 years. The values were presented in mission statements, vision statements and, ultimately, a theme. The vision statement, which provided a natural conclusion to Envisioning Laurier, was as follows:

Our commitment is to justice and sustainability now and in the future, so we strive to ignite the minds, spirits and hearts of our communities through excellence in teaching and learning, in the discovery, scholarly exploration, and application of new ideas, and in instilling the courage to engage and challenge the world in all its complexity.

The mission statement was more detailed, and concluded with the Latin phrase that had long been the university's motto:

Wilfrid Laurier University strives to be a diverse, personal and supportive community. It is devoted to learning, research, scholarship, creativity, professional expertise and personal development in a student-centred environment. Faculty and staff work with highly talented undergraduate, master's and doctoral students, and other individuals interested in lifelong learning. Our aim is to educate engaged and aware citizens of an increasingly complex world. The Laurier community fulfills this mission through distinctive programs in arts and social sciences, business and economics, music, science, social work and theology.

Veritas Omnia Vincit. (Truth Conquers All)

Discussing the process, President Blouw remarked that while every university aims for academic excellence, devotion to research and scholarship, it was important to define what set Laurier apart. The answer was found in a six-word phrase that defined not only the goal of Laurier but, in the opinion of many participants, the characteristics that defined it: *"Inspiring lives of leadership and purpose."*

To Dr. Blouw, the phrase encompassed the real strength of Laurier, an institution that values academic learning but also encourages students, faculty, staff and alumni to take a leadership role in all aspects of their lives.

There was, and is, more to the exercise than simply creating appealing statements and polished promises. The most important outcome is the collection of submissions and documents reflecting the hopes of the current generation of academics and support staff for the school's future, in other words the benchmarks needed to assess decisions made and action taken over the next three decades.

Inspiring lives of leadership and purpose will always be a challenge. It was clearly the unstated goal of the group that banded together to found the seminary in 1911, and remains the goal today. It was easier to create a sense of common commitment in the early days and more difficult as enrolment approaches the 20,000 threshold. Envisioning Laurier laid the groundwork and provides direction as the university works to maintain what made Laurier unique while also embracing the potential of its future.

Laurier might not yet have achieved the status of a comprehensive university, but it clearly is no longer a small liberal arts college. As Blouw says, the school continues to retain the spirit and sense of community that marked the earlier period. The challenge going forward will be to maintain that spirit and connection as Laurier enters its second century. The university's current five-year Academic Plan, which succeeded the previous Century Plan in 2011, attempts to address some of these challenges. While the classroom experience remains important, the new plan focuses on an increased role for research across the university. Emphasis on research will be accompanied, however, by an increased commitment to what the school calls "the integrated and engaged learning model." This model involves not just the traditional co-op programs but further integration of academic curriculum with co-curricular work and general community involvement.

Throughout its history, Wilfrid Laurier University found ways to not simply survive but to thrive. It confronted the challenges of too few students and occasionally has had to meet the challenge of too many. Firmly anchored to its past, it has not been afraid, especially recently, to embrace new methods and new ideas to accomplish the goals that define it.

ABOVE: Shinerama, one of the Laurier student body's annual demonstrations of leadership and purpose.

As it goes forward to face challenging attitudes toward higher education, Laurier can take comfort in the knowledge that it has always found the path to success. Persistence and ambition has brought Laurier to a place in the front rank of Canada's institutions of higher learning.

ABOVE: The amphitheatre on the Waterloo campus, 2011.

ℰDUCATE or 𝒟IE!

WHERE are the young men of today who will be the Lutheran pastors of tomorrow? · · · They are in our Lutheran Colleges. studying, learning and growing, to prepare for the spiritual leadership ahead of them.

Suppose we had no Lutheran Colleges; where would they be? Nowhere; there would be practically no Lutheran pastors for the future.

Ninety-two per cent, of all the educated men in the Christian ministry have been educated in the colleges of their own denomination, 9 of every 10 educated Baptist ministers come from Baptist colleges; 9 of every 10 educated Anglican ministers come from Anglican colleges; 9 of every 10 educated Lutheran ministers come from Lutheran colleges, and so on in every denomination.

St. John's Evangelical Lutheran Church
Waterloo, Ont.

Each Church body must educate its own ministers or go without educated ministers. We must "educate or die."

A Church body which ignores or evades its duty to educate, sooner or later drops out of the service of the Master. Look back over the history of the Christian Church and see the fate of

CONCLUSION
EDUCATE OR DIE!

IN 1929, AMIDST ONE OF THE MANY financial crises faced by Waterloo College, a pamphlet was published with the hyperbolic title *Educate or Die!* directed at those who wished to support a domestically educated Lutheran ministry. It carried the warning that without support for the college and seminary, not just a ministry but the church itself might be destroyed.

The phrase serves as a means to encapsulate the history of the institution. Almost from its inception in 1911, and throughout each of its various incarnations, Wilfrid Laurier University saw the drive to educate more and more young people as a means to survive and develop.

In the dark days of the First World War, the seminary recognized the need to create high school courses for under-qualified applicants. Those classes were later supplemented by college courses which, in turn, necessitated the negotiation of an affiliation with the University of Western Ontario. The alternative seemed to be destruction or at least dramatic reduction of the institution. Similar arguments could be made for the first admission of female students in 1929, a measure that not only expanded the student body, but further ingrained the college and seminary in the community of Waterloo.

In the years of the Great Depression and the Second World War, the need for more enrolment drove the decisions of university administrators, while in the heady days after the Second World War, providing teaching and residence facilities, not recruiting, became the problem. Faced with the challenge, Waterloo College raced down the road of expansion.

The decision not to become part of the University of Waterloo might appear a brief departure from this trend, but in fact the decision to educate in the way the college thought appropriate was at the root of the decision and, in 1960, Waterloo College became Waterloo Lutheran University. The determination to educate and not to die lived on.

By 1973, Waterloo Lutheran University's ability to educate was severely restricted by its limited access to provincial funds. Again the decision was made to survive and to educate. Going forward as Wilfrid Laurier University, the institution found itself tied to increasing enrolment to fund the expansion of programs and buildings that the university needed to compete in the modern academic world. While the alternative was, perhaps, no longer institutional death, success and prominence in the academic community would rely on educating ever-increasing numbers of undergraduates.

The modern period of government cutbacks contrasted with the demand for new, more costly facilities. Laurier had to expand to compete. It chose to grow from one campus to two, incorporating more distance and continuing-education programs to move into the ranks of mid-sized Canadian universities.

The dramatic phrase *Educate Or Die* also encapsulates the spirit of the Lutheran Church in Canada. Over more than 60 years, it invested Herculean amounts of energy, money and determination in an effort to maintain the college it created. As well, the phrase symbolizes generations of determined faculty, staff and administrators who worked desperately to ensure the educational standard and success of Laurier and its predecessors.

It hints as well at the conviction of the communities in which Laurier is based. The decades of support that the people of Waterloo, Kitchener and the surrounding region invested in Waterloo College and the university, were supplemented recently by the outstanding efforts of the City of Brantford to attract, construct and maintain a university campus in its community.

The challenge implicit in the bold, three-word title of the 1929 fundraising pamphlet has been met time and again by Wilfrid Laurier University, Waterloo Lutheran University and the seminary and college that preceded it. As it moves forward, the university will build on that spirit, sacrifice and resolve which made the long, ultimately impressive history of the institution possible.

ABOVE: A popular image of Sir Wilfrid Laurier used on banners, advertisements and publications during the university's centennial year.

LEADERSHIP AND PURPOSE

WRITING ABOUT LAURIER

I N THE COURSE OF ITS HISTORY, Wilfrid Laurier University and its predecessor
institutions attracted the attention of authors on more than one occasion. This brief
discussion looks at some writings that were influential in the construction of this book.

The Waterloo Historical Society's annual publication on occasion has turned its attention
to Waterloo College, the forerunner of the modern Wilfrid Laurier University. In 1949,
Alex Potter wrote an article on the history of the school to celebrate its 25-year affiliation
with the University of Western Ontario. In 1986, Laurier Librarian Eric Schultz wrote
a related article detailing the 75-year history of the institution. To their discussions, both
authors brought the personal perspectives of long careers spent at the institution.

In the society's 2007 volume, two articles on the history of Wilfrid Laurier University appear. The first, entitled *The Intruders: the Impact of Co-education on Waterloo College between the Years 1929-1939,* written by Natalie Rubino, examines the admission and influence of women at the college. In the same volume, Rych Mills writes about reaction to the decision to admit women and also the fundraising efforts that accompanied it. His article is entitled *The Circle of Its Usefulness: How Kitchener-Waterloo Learned of the 1929 Changes at Waterloo College.*

In 2000, University of Toronto Press published a volume edited by Barbara Austin called *Capitalizing Knowledge: Essays on the History of Business Education,* a series of papers presented at the Administrative Sciences Association of Canada's annual conference in 1999. John McCutcheon and Bob Ellis contributed an article entitled *The Evolution of Management Education in a Small Canadian University: the School of Business and Economics of Wilfrid Laurier University.* Their paper provided an invaluable discussion of the history of business education at Laurier, placing its development in the context of national circumstances.

In 1991, Dr. Shankar A. Yelaja, dean of social work at the time, wrote *Celebrating 25 Years: A History of the Faculty of Social Work, Wilfrid Laurier University, 1966-1991,* which outlines the history of that faculty.

The 75th anniversary of Wilfrid Laurier University and the Lutheran Seminary created a number of publications focused on its history. *Laurier: A Photographic History,* by Arthur Stephen and Douglas Ratchford, provides a photo-rich overview. Debbie Lou Ludolph edited and designed *By Faith We Walk: a Pictorial History of Waterloo Lutheran Seminary,* which is a rich pictorial record of the seminary's development. The most detailed academic investigation of the seminary was written by historian Dr. Oscar Cole-Arnal: *Towards an Indigenous Lutheran Ministry in Canada: the 75-Year Pilgrimage of Waterloo Lutheran Seminary (1911-1986)* examines every aspect of the creation and development of the seminary, focusing on faculty, the student body and institutional issues.

In 1971, Barry Lyon published *The First 60 Years: A History of Waterloo Lutheran University from the Opening of Waterloo Lutheran Seminary in 1911, to the Present Day.* Dr. Flora Roy published two volumes of memoirs related to the university, the first dealing with Waterloo College, the second when the institution was called Waterloo Lutheran University. These two volumes are available online through Laurier's Library.

The tumultuous circumstances surrounding the creation of the University of Waterloo and the fracture between that institution and Waterloo Lutheran University are dealt with in magnificent fashion by Waterloo historian Dr. Kenneth McLaughlin in his book, *Waterloo: the Unconventional Founding of an Unconventional University.* McLaughlin's interviews, research and detailed approach make the very complex subject much more accessible. McLaughlin was also very kind in sharing material with the author of this book.

The creation and expansion of Wilfrid Laurier University's Brantford campus is dealt with at length by Dr. Leo Groarke in his book *Reinventing Brantford: The University Comes Downtown.* Groarke, the second dean and first principal of the Brantford campus, wrote a very personal discussion of the trials and tribulations of launching a new campus in difficult circumstances.

All of these articles and volumes are supplemented by the wonderful facilities of the Laurier Archives. Its rich collection and very helpful staff make possible virtually any task in examining the university's past. The collection includes not only the complete run of *The Cord*, but also documents, publications and photographs from throughout the university's history.